I0029252

Infinite Learning
Diversity

Other Books by Author

Overcome Any Obstacle to Creativity

Infinite Learning Diversity

Uncovering the Hidden Talents of Our Students

Tony McCaffrey

ROWMAN & LITTLEFIELD
Lanham • Boulder • New York • London

Published by Rowman & Littlefield
An imprint of The Rowman & Littlefield Publishing Group, Inc.
4501 Forbes Boulevard, Suite 200, Lanham, Maryland 20706
www.rowman.com

6 Tinworth Street, London SE11 5AL, United Kingdom

Copyright © 2019 by Tony McCaffrey

All rights reserved. No part of this book may be reproduced in any form or by any electronic or mechanical means, including information storage and retrieval systems, without written permission from the publisher, except by a reviewer who may quote passages in a review.

British Library Cataloguing in Publication Information Available

Library of Congress Cataloging-in-Publication Data Is Available

ISBN 978-1-4758-3460-4 (cloth: alk. paper)
ISBN 978-1-4758-3461-1 (pbk: alk. paper)
ISBN 978-1-4758-3462-8 (electronic)

♾™ The paper used in this publication meets the minimum requirements of American National Standard for Information Sciences—Permanence of Paper for Printed Library Materials, ANSI/NISO Z39.48-1992.

To my boss and the thought leader of Eagle Hill School (EHS), Dr. Michael Riendeau, and my EHS students. Michael hired me and from the first day has inspired, supported, and encouraged me to apply everything I know about cognitive psychology and neuroscience to the benefit of our students. My students have taught me much about being human, especially the truly diverse ways of not only "thinking outside the box" but "living outside the box." May my students continue to defy all the boxes we try to put them in. And may the framework of Infinite Learning Diversity not just be a larger set of boxes, but a rich, descriptive way to honor, respect, and facilitate their diverse and unique ways of being.

Contents

Preface

Studying Cognition Correctly?

ANIMAL COGNITION

In *Are We Smart Enough to Know How Smart Animals Are?*, Frans de Waal discusses how the study of animal cognition is recently breaking free of lumping diverse animals into one category and judging them on one dimension of intelligence. Before this recent shift, researchers would often give the same puzzles to diverse species without any accommodations. For example, chimps easily use long sticks to reach up for elevated food, but elephants do not. Are chimps therefore smarter than elephants? Not if you notice that an elephant does not pick up sticks with the tip of its trunk because the stick would block its nasal passage. Replace the stick with a sturdy box and the elephant will kick the box into position so it can stand on it to retrieve the food.

Similarly, macaques can solve a particular string puzzle, but gibbons cannot. The temptation is to conclude that macaques are smarter than gibbons until you realize that gibbons, without fully opposable thumbs, do not have the dexterity to pick up a string from the ground. Hang the string in mid-air and gibbons easily grab it to solve the problem.

Instead of asking which animals are smarter than others are, de Waal asks whether human researchers are smart enough to evaluate how smart different animals are. In other words, are humans smart enough to properly investigate animal intelligence?

HUMAN COGNITION

The same can be asked of many of our schools. With standardized tests and narrow appraisals of success still being used, are school officials really that far ahead of animal cognition researchers when it comes to handling the immense cognitive diversity within the human species?

Chimpanzees look very different than elephants, so it is fairly easy to imagine that they have different abilities. We humans, however, generally look very similar to each other, so it is harder to imagine the diversity of our inner experiences. Further, since most people can use a language to communicate with others in that same language, again it is easy to project that their inner lives are very similar to ours. Our similar appearance and similar use of language mask the rich diversity that hides within each of us. If our externalized lives through language are understandable to others who use the same language, then shouldn't our inner lives be pretty much the same? This is what we often assume, but our assumption is highly inaccurate.

We need to take the next step to articulate and appreciate the immense diversity of our mental life.

REFERENCE

de Waal, F. (2017). *Are We Smart Enough to Know How Smart Animals Are?* New York: W. W. Norton & Company.

Introduction

The time has come for a more extensive theory of human cognitive abilities that takes into account the latest neuroscience and theories of cognitive evolution. Howard Gardner's *Multiple Intelligences* took great strides to open us up to the diverse abilities of the human person. But naturally, we now know more about the mind and the brain since the 1980s when *Multiple Intelligences* was first introduced. This book on *Infinite Learning Diversity* is one attempt to take another stride forward in appreciating the immense cognitive diversity of the human person.

This need became clear to me when I began to teach at Eagle Hill School (EHS) (www.eaglehill.school), a school for students with learning differences. The theories that I had learned about while finishing my doctorate in cognitive psychology were unable to describe, let alone explain, the diversity of cognitive abilities that I witnessed at EHS on a daily basis. The many results of neuroscience that I learned had not yet been assembled in a way that I could easily apply to the abilities that I saw in my students.

For example, the thick educational and neuropsychological file on my student John (a pseudonym) gave no indication of his exceptional ability to manipulate and easily disentangle the parts of the most difficult entangled metal puzzles on the market. The file and poor math grades of my student Connor (a pseudonym) gave no indication that he would be able to solve a math problem called the *Konigsberg Bridge problem* in five minutes, which was originally solved by the most prolific mathematician of all time, Leonhard Euler. This one problem launched a whole new branch of mathematics. The stories continue in this book of the exceptional abilities that I have witnessed in my three short years at EHS.

Who else's abilities was I missing? I was working in an *ad hoc* manner by giving my students puzzles of various sorts. I needed a systematic framework to help me see the landscape of these abilities. Why were the current academic and psychological assessments missing these abilities? I looked at their theoretical underpinnings and found generally that they have very few categories (visual, auditory, kinesthetic, etc.) for these abilities to fit into. I needed a richer vocabulary.

So, in the framework presented in this book, I went to the other extreme looking for abilities among all the different features that humans can detect with our senses (e.g., color, symmetry, and texture) and all the differences we can think about with our minds. A person could have a very specific ability to be extraordinary in detecting and manipulating any one of these features. In contrast, a person might be very poor at or even unable to detect and manipulate another particular feature.

Maybe my current framework is too extensive and fine-grained and will need to be curtailed. But given the small number of categories of current theories, I wanted to err on the side of being too expansive and all-encompassing. There is currently an unlimited number of features within this current framework and I have mathematically proven that no computer can list out all the unlimited features of a physical object (McCaffrey and Spector, 2017).

In addition to an extensive set of features, the framework articulated in this book also deals with the many ways we tend to group these features (inspired by Gestalt psychologists) and other ways that we combine these features into a unified and coherent thing (inspired by *conceptual blending* from Fauconnier and Turner, 2002). Again, a person might have an exceptional ability or a complete inability to group features in a certain way or combine/unify features in a certain manner.

Further, a particular feature may focus the attention of a particular person and diffuse the attention of another person.

As you can imagine, all the combinations of a person's ability (or inability) to detect and manipulate various features, group them, combine/unify them, and attend to them lead to an extensive and rich way to describe a person's abilities. The unlimited nature of this new framework led to the choice of the suggestive word *Infinite* in the term *Infinite Learning Diversity*.

In sum, *Infinite Learning Diversity* is an extensive framework with multiple moving parts. This book motivates the need for a new framework; articulates the basic framework; describes how more abilities can be unearthed using this framework than with current theories; articulates how more struggles in learning and understanding can be detected and counteracted; and shows multiple case studies of exceptional abilities that were either previously undetected, under-appreciated, or unexplained.

INVITATION TO COLLABORATE

This *Infinite Learning Diversity* framework needs much work to be refined and tested. I invite any interested teacher, administrator, parent, student advocate, student, or researcher to join in on the process. Our youth have some amazing abilities that either go undetected or undeveloped. A new, extensive framework based on the latest neuroscience can help us see, appreciate, and develop many more of these abilities. Our youth also struggle with some mystifying learning and comprehensions issues. A new, expansive framework can help explain those issues and suggest ways to address them.

Please contact me if you would like to be part of this endeavor that flows from the *Infinite Learning Diversity* approach or you would like me to be a part of your work of noticing, appreciating, and nurturing the awe-inspiring cognitive diversity of our students.

Email: tmccaffrey@eaglehill.school

REFERENCES

Fauconnier, G. & Turner, M. (2002). *The way we think: Conceptual blending and the mind's hidden complexities.* Basic Books.

Gardner, H. (1993). *Frames of mind: The theory of multiple intelligences.* New York: Basic Books.

McCaffrey, T., & Spector, L. (2017). An approach to human–machine collaboration in innovation. *Artificial Intelligence for Engineering Design, Analysis and Manufacturing*, 1–15. doi:10.1017/S0890060416000524.

Chapter 1

Problem

Few Categories and Missing Neuroscience

INTRODUCTION

This book will be using the term *learning diversity* but there is an emerging term, *neurodiversity*, that will be considered to be synonymous.

Although the emerging field is called *neurodiversity*, surprisingly, there has yet to be a neural grounding to this field. Further, the number of categories to describe the diversity of cognitive abilities is currently fairly small. This chapter fleshes out these two current limitations which set the stage for how to overcome them. Ground a new framework in neuroscience and craft a richly extensive number of categories to describe small differences in cognitive abilities.

CURRENT NON-NEURAL BASES TO NEURODIVERSITY

Neurodiversity is an emerging field that focuses on the diverse ways to be human based on differences in the neurological system. Ironically, in expressing neural diversity, this young field currently, as described by Armstrong (2012), relies upon category schemes that come only from neighboring fields around neuroscience: education (Dunn and Dunn's learning style approach: Dunn & Dunn, 1992), business (Clifton StrengthsFinder: Gallup Youth Development Specialists, 2007), developmental psychology (Search Institute's Developmental Assets framework: Benson, 1997), and behavioral psychology (Multiple Intelligences: Gardner, 1993; Myers-Briggs Type Indicator: Myers, 1995). No category scheme has yet to emerge from neuroscience itself (Armstrong, 2012).

CURRENT SMALL CATEGORY SYSTEMS

Each of the current category schemes for neurodiversity mentioned by Armstrong has a relatively small number of categories. Here are the present category schemes and their number of categories: Dunn and Dunn's learning style approach (18 categories; Dunn and Dunn, 1992), Clifton Strengths-Finder (34 categories; Gallup Youth Development Specialists, 2007), Search Institute's Developmental Assets framework (40 categories; Benson, 1997), Multiple Intelligences (at most 10 categories; Gardner, 1993), Myers-Briggs Type Indicator (16 categories; Myers, 1995), and Armstrong (170 categories; 2012) itself.

Below are the details of each category scheme mentioned in Armstrong.

Dunn and Dunn's learning style approach uses five major categories with sub-categories within each one for a total of 18 options: Environment (Sound, Light, Temperature, and Seating Design), Emotional (Motivational support, Persistence, Individual Responsibility, and Structure), Sociological (Individual, Pairs or Teams, and Adult Varied), Physiological (Perceptual Intake, Time, and Mobility), Psychological (Global, Analytical, Impulsive, and Reflective) (Dunn and Dunn, 1992).

Clifton StrengthsFinder (Gallup Youth Development Specialists, 2007) uses 34 categories: Achiever, Activator, Adaptability, Analytical, Arranger, Belief, Command, Communication, Competition, Connectedness, Consistency/Fairness, Context, Deliberative, Developer, Discipline, Empathy, Focus, Futuristic, Harmony, Ideation, Inclusiveness/Includer, Individualization, Input, Intellection, Learner, Maximizer, Positivity, Relator, Responsibility, Restorative, Self-Assurance, Significance, Strategic, and Woo.

Search Institute's Developmental Assets framework (Benson, 1997) has two major categories (i.e., external assets and internal assets), which have various subcategories for a total of 40 options: External Assets: Family Support, Positive Family Communication, Other Adult Relationships, Caring Neighborhood, Caring School Climate, Parent Involvement in Schooling, Community Values Youth, Youth as Resources, Service to Others, Safety, Family Boundaries, School Boundaries, Neighborhood Boundaries, Adult Role Models, Positive Peer Influence, High Expectations, Creative Activities, Youth Programs, Religious Community, Time at Home; Internal Assets: Achievement Motivation, School Engagement, Homework, Bonding to School, Reading for Pleasure, Caring, Equality and Social Justice, Integrity, Honesty, Responsibility, Restraint, Planning and Decision Making, Interpersonal Competence, Cultural Competence, Resistance Skills, Peaceful Conflict Resolution, Personal Power, Self-Esteem, Sense of Purpose, and Positive View of Personal Future.

Multiple Intelligences initially started with eight categories but Gardner eventually suggested two more: musical–rhythmic, visual-spatial, verbal-linguistic, logical–mathematical, bodily–kinesthetic, interpersonal, intrapersonal, and naturalistic (Gardner, 1993). Gardner has since then suggested that existential and moral intelligences are also possible candidates.

Myers-Briggs Type Indicator presents four categories each with two options for a total of 16 options: extraversion, introversion; sensing, intuition; thinking, feeling; judgment, perception (Myers, 1995).

Armstrong (2012) created his own checklist of strengths consisting of 17 categories and a total of 165 options: Personal, Communication, Social, Emotional, Cognitive, Creative, Literacy, Logical, Visual-Spatial, Physical, Dexterity, Musical, Nature, High-Tech, Spiritual, Cultural, and Other. Cognitive strengths include "Has good study skills," "Is able to think ahead," and "Has a good short-term or long-term memory." Creativity strengths include "Has a good imagination," "Enjoys doodling, drawing, or painting," and "Comes up with ideas that nobody else has thought of."

SUMMARY

The two main weaknesses of current cognitive theories are that they are not thoroughly grounded in neuroscience and they use relatively few categories when describing human cognitive abilities. The next chapter will begin the grounding in neuroscience by examining a ubiquitous mental operation that most of us take for granted.

REFERENCES

Armstrong, T. (2012). *Neurodiversity in the classroom: Strength-based strategies to help students with special needs succeed in school and life.* Alexandria, VA: ASCD.

Benson, P. L. (1997). *All kids are our kids: What communities must do to raise caring and responsible children and adolescents.* New York: Jossey-Bass.

Dunn, R., & Dunn, K. (1992). *Teaching elementary students through their individual learning style.* Boston: Allyn & Bacon.

Gallup Youth Development Specialists. (2007). *Strengths explorer for ages 10 to 14* (2nd ed.). Washington, DC: Gallup Press.

Gardner, H. (1993). *Frames of mind: The theory of multiple intelligences.* New York: Basic Books.

Myers, I. B. (1995). *Gifts differing: Understanding personality type.* Boston: Nicholas Brealey Publishing.

Chapter 2

A Mammal Thought Experiment

INTRODUCTION

In order to ground this new framework in neuroscience, an evolutionary thought experiment will be presented that helps us envision the range of possible relationships between perception and memory. At one end of the spectrum, they operate very independently with either perception or memory dominating the brain's activity at any one time. At the other end, perception and memory can be blended together to form neural activity that presents a fiction that has never been experienced.

Perhaps, there was a time when our evolutionary ancestors could be in either a perceptual state or a memory state. Then, random associations and intrusions came on the scene. Then, some ancestors began to be able to control how perception and memory blended to produce useful fictions that could help them solve problems. From this perspective, language would serve as a great tool to guide and control this blending for useful purposes.

This chapter presents the thought experiment and chapter 4 presents the underlying neuroscience that makes it plausible.

THINKING WITHOUT LANGUAGE

How did we humans think before we acquired language? How do non-human mammals think and solve problems without language? Here is a simple thought experiment that sets the stage for what much of the research in neuroscience is pointing toward.

Two small mammals live on a savanna some distance from each other many millions of years ago. The first mammal comes out of its hole to forage for food. After traveling some distance, it eats a couple small berries and then spots a large peach-like piece of fruit on the ground. It nudges and rolls the fruit back home. When the fruit gets close to the hole, it picks up speed and rolls ahead of the mammal. The fruit is too big and blocks the entrance to the hole. Fear and panic shoot through the mammal as it suddenly feels completely vulnerable to predators because it cannot get into its hole. While it bites and scratches at the fruit, other mammals inside the hole push the fruit free and the fruit is abandoned for the safety of the hole (Figure 2.1).

The mammal has a sophisticated perceptual system and vivid memories, but it cannot combine them. When observing the fruit, it can only consider the perception of the fruit in front of it or the memory of its distant hole. In this way, it was unable to assess whether or not the fruit might fit in the hole that it could not see. It could not bring together its perception of the fruit with its memory of the hole. Even if the mammal switched back and forth between the perception and the memory, still it may not yield an accurate assessment.

From another hole far from the first, another mammal emerges to look for food. Something is different about this mammal. It has the same basic perceptual system as the first mammal. It also has vivid memories. However, this mammal can blend together what it is perceiving with what it is remembering to create an experience-of-sorts that it has never actually experienced.

This mammal also finds and eats a couple berries, then locates a peach-like piece of fruit to bring back home. The large piece is tempting because of its size, but the perception of the fruit combined with a flash of a memory of

Figure 2.1 Panicked Mammal with Food Blocking Hole. *Source*: Natasha Sharpe drew this illustration and the author purchased it for use by Roman & Littlefield in this book.

her home hole unleashes a tinge of fear in her as she momentarily "views" the large fruit blocking her home hole. She moves past the large fruit to find something smaller, which she nudges back home and into the hole where all there can feast (Figure 2.2).

The power to blend perception with memory in order to make assessments ultimately has survival value. This blending ability is crucial for possessing a cognitive system that can creatively solve important, live-saving problems. This position initially seems counterintuitive since we might think that it would always be more desirable for our neural states to accurately portray what is being perceived. However, producing something fictional based on perception and memory can be crucial for solving problems and ultimately for survival.

By blending, we mean that the neural activity triggered by what is perceived is combined with the neural activity initiated from a retrieved memory. The result is a state of neural activity that presents a fiction—something not actually experienced. The more the animal can initiate and control the proper blends, the better they can solve important problems for themselves and their kin.

Notice that for this case of problem-solving, we did not need to posit that the mammal possessed a specialized area of the brain for analysis or a public

Figure 2.2 Blending Perception and Memory to Solve a Problem. *Source*: Natasha Sharpe drew this illustration and the author purchased it for use by Roman & Littlefield in this book.

language. All we had to do was soften the border between perception and memory to produce a system that can imagine scenes that have not happened. Suddenly, it can look into possible futures. But, it can do more than that. It can produce any fiction, including scenes that cannot ever happen.

In sum, blending the past (memory) and the present (perception) produces a huge advancement in cognitive ability. Chapter 3 motivates how blends happen in humans, sometimes in spite of our language abilities. Chapter 4 presents the neuroscience behind this thought experiment and makes this simple thought experiment more realistic and nuanced. There are many ways that the brain can soften the boundary between perception and memory and mix the two.

But briefly, first, where does language fit overall into this evolutionary picture? Language seems to come on the scene much more recently in evolutionary terms than blending of perceptions and memories. We will look at animal examples of problem-solving in which there are very few interpretations possible that do not include blending of some sort.

From this perspective, one thing language does is to help control and guide the blendings that are taking place within the brain. With language, you can also trigger a blend in another that they might never create on their own. In this way, language serves as a way to trigger and guide the blending process.

Before moving ahead on the motivation behind and neuroscience beneath blending, let us first put blending in perspective by examining multiple ways that a person might solve a problem that does not necessarily involve blending.

EYELETS IN A HIGH-TOP BASKETBALL SHOE

How many eyelets does a high-top basketball sneaker generally have? Eyelets are the holes that the shoelaces go through. First, we need language in order to couch an accurate answer, so this problem is for a linguistic being. The main reason we need language is that we are dealing with precise numbers above three. As the research described below shows, dealing with more than three items is problematic for all that have been tested: pre-linguistic children, adults who use languages with either no number words or very few, primates, and some birds.

If you as a human being have inquired about the number of eyelets before, then you can just use your memory to retrieve the answer. A previous inquiry ensued, in philosopher John Dewey's terms, and the matter is now *settled*. The answer might already be encoded in a linguistic form. In this case, answering the question does not require constructing an image but just retrieving the number in a linguistic form.

If this is a new *unsettled* inquiry, then you could use analysis to deduce that it must be an even number. There is the same number of eyelets on each side of the shoe. Analysis can help constrain the possible answer. Based on forming an image from memory of a single shoe you have experienced or a composite image based on shoes you have experienced, you could estimate a range of possible eyelets for the high-top sneaker. If you do not have a clear memory of a particular shoe, then forming a composite shoe from multiple examples could be considered a form of blending. You are piecing together one shoe based on multiple shoes you have experienced.

You could also use analysis to infer that a high-top shoe might be about twice as high as a normal shoe, so they are probably about twice as many eyelets as a normal shoe. Consequently, you could estimate based on shoe height that the answer is probably between twelve and twenty.

The analysis part of this process requires being aware of symmetry, precise numbers above three, the evenness and oddness of numbers, the relative height of low cut and high top shoes. A linguistic species could use language to help it focus upon the connections between symmetry and evenness or the connection between twice the height and twice the number of eyelets.

If you have never seen a high-top basketball sneaker before, then a linguistic description may be needed to guide your construction of an image. Imagine a shoe with a shoestring, but the shoe extends above your ankle to give it more support for quick turning. This basic description should be able to guide you to an estimate. If normal shoes have four to six eyelets, then extending them above your ankles might yield between eight and twelve. Of course, language is needed in this case to trigger the construction of the image of an object that the person has never experienced before.

The brain will tend to engage in the most efficient—least energy consuming—way to answer the question. Remembering a fact of how many eyelets are on a high-top sneaker is probably more energy efficient than generating an image. Of course, we can force ourselves to carefully image a high-top shoe and spend a great deal of time and energy answering the question.

In sum, there are many ways to solve this problem and four basic possibilities have been presented: retrieve a linguistic fact if the problem has been solved before, combine analysis of symmetry with an image, combine analysis of relative height with images of regular shoes and high-top shoes, retrieve an image of a high-top shoe and make an estimate, and construct an image based on a description of a regular tie shoe that extends above the ankle. Not all of these require blending. But blending is an amazing ability that we often take for granted. Some people are better at it than others, as we will see in the next section.

THE UBIQUITY OF BLENDING

In the field of linguistics, Fauconnier and Turner (2002, 2003) have articulated a theory called *Conceptual Blending*, which is a general cognitive capacity to mix elements from different domains into one coherent domain. According to these authors and others, Conceptual Blending undergirds many cognitive abilities including analogy making, metaphor, problem-solving, and language. The words and grammar of a language act as triggers of loose instructions for how to blend together the diverse content into a coherent scenario.

Humans probably engage in Conceptual Blending many times throughout our day. The list below touches upon just a few of the diverse set of mundane activities that could be answered by a blending process. Of course, there are always other ways to address these questions.

During furniture shopping, will the couch in front of you look good in your living room?

During furniture shopping, with the couch in front of you fit in your living room?

During shopping, will the outfit in the store window look good on your child? Blend the perception of the outfit with the memory of your child.

Will the leftovers on the stove behind you fit in the plastic container you are viewing in the kitchen cupboard in front of you?

Will your car fit in that tight parking spot?

Will the tangled extension cord reach the outlet once you untangle it?

How many people will fit in the front pew of your church?

When at the grocery store, which side of the car should you put your groceries on so they will be closest to the front door when you arrive back home?

How many trips will it take to carry in the groceries from your car?

How will you arrange the suitcases to fit in your car before you head to the airport?

Will your carry-on luggage fit in the overhead compartment? (People are bad at this task—maybe sometimes on purpose.)

Will the bowl of mashed potatoes feed everyone at the dinner table?

Will the neighbor's van fit in your garage?

A few comments on a few of these questions. *Will the couch in front of you look good in your living room?* This could be answered based just on knowing which colors go with other colors. So, no full image of the couch in your living room is required. *Will the couch in front of you fit in your living room?* This could be answered based on knowing the fact that your current couch is the longest one that will fit in your living room. Based on that, the couch in front of you could be compared to the size of your own body. You imagine yourself lying down on the couch and it seems to be the about the same size—which involves blending. Or, you actually lie down on the couch in the store. Or, you measure it. Or, you just blend and approximate that it seems to be the same size as your couch at home.

So, each question can be addressed in several ways, some of which do not involve blending. Some involve our spatial sense more than others and these involve how our proprioceptive abilities know the position of our body in space, its distance from other objects around us, and the position of our body parts (e.g., arms and legs) relative to our own body.

Before continuing, however, we will briefly look at our abilities in numerical cognition that make determining the number of eyelets in a high-top shoe a challenging question.

NUMBERS ABOVE THREE

Caleb Everett, in his book *Numbers and the Making of Us*, argues that quantities are natural for us to be aware of (e.g., a little, a lot). Handling the basics of quantities does not require language. However, numbers are not natural to us and require a language to name and manipulate properly.

Not every human language has words for numbers. The Piraha people of the Amazon have no words for precise numbers, not even for one. (Everett, 2018). Careful testing shows that as the number of objects presented start at one and are increased the Piraha generally use one word but its use gradually fades and another word is used as the items increase. Importantly, there were individual differences in when one person changed over to the use of a new word. Consequently, the first word used is generally translated as a "small amount" and the second word as a "few." The words referred to an inexact range of items and that range differed for different people. Interestingly, the same conclusions hold for young children as they grow up with languages that have precise numbers for many—even infinite—numbers. Young children start at this imprecise level before they can precisely name the number of items presented to them.

The Munduruku people, also of the Amazon, in contrast, do have precise words for groups of one and two items. However, their words for three and four items are not always used in a precise manner. Beyond four, approximate words are used that are generally translated as "some" and "many."

The best current understanding of all the data from the Piraha, the Munduruka, and pre-linguistic children is that humans have two numerical senses. First, humans have an ability to estimate quantities and even infants can recognize large differences in two quantities—that there is a difference between ten items and twenty items, for example. Generally, it seems if there is a 2:1 ratio or more between two groups of items then pre-linguistic children can register that there is a difference. It gets problematic, however, when the ratio is less than 2:1.

Second, it seems that humans have an innate capacity to differentiate between one item, two items, and three items. These are the quantities that we can ascertain immediately without counting or grouping together sub-groups of the items.

This ability is called *subitizing*. There are disagreements among experimental results on the most items that humans can subitize. Different results have shown the limit at three, four, and five. There may be individual differences in our ability to subitize, also. Further, it is tricky to test. If a person is familiar with dice, then they immediately recognize the number six. However, if six dots are randomly placed, then they will probably need to count. If a random group of six dots is close to the pattern on dice, then no counting may be necessary. Further, the person may be able to group a random pattern of six dots quickly into sub-groups of four and two, or three and three. This quick grouping may be so fast that it appears that they are not grouping or counting.

The best current interpretation of the experiments with the Piraha is that their ability to estimate quantities is intact while their ability to subitize seems somehow to be influenced by the lack of precise names for small numbers. Until further research is done, this seems to be a most plausible hypothesis.

SUMMARY

The thought experiment lays the groundwork for a powerful mental ability to blend together perception and memory (or multiple memories). Blending could be performed by non-linguistic animals. It is important to keep distinguishing which tasks require language and which do not. This will not only help us appreciate and more accurately assess non-linguistic animals. But it will also help us understand the impact that language has on human cognition—both positive and negative. As in the case of numbers, non-linguistic animals can still successfully work with quantities and three or fewer items.

The next chapter, chapter 3, looks at some human experiences without language as a way to continue to motivate the ongoing need to assess what language does to our cognitive abilities. Chapter 4 presents the underlying neuroscience of perception, memory, and how blending may have evolved as a cognitive ability. Language is reintroduced and addressed starting in chapter 5 as to how it might relate to our underlying non-linguistic cognitive abilities—especially, blending.

REFERENCES

Everett, C. (2017). *Numbers and the making of us.* Cambridge, MA: Harvard University Press.

Fauconnier, G. & Turner, M. (2002). *The way we think: Conceptual blending and the mind's hidden complexities.* Basic Books.

Fauconnier, G. & Turner, M. (2003). Conceptual blending, form and meaning. *Recherches en Communication, 19*, 57–86.

Chapter 3

More Non-linguistic Experiences with Blending

THE CHIMP AND THE PEANUT

Consider a chimp that has a long, clear tube secured to its cage door. At the bottom of the tube is a peanut that, of course, the chimp wants to eat. For ten minutes, the chimp sticks its fingers down the tube, which are too short, and tries to pull the tube from the cage door, which it cannot do. Then suddenly, the chimp leaves the tube and returns with a mouthful of water, which it spits into the tube. The peanut floats upwards within the chimp's reach and a snack is served! You can see a chimp solve this problem at https://www.youtube.com/watch?v=yrPb41hzYdw.

Amazing! The solution took ten minutes so it was not obvious or trivial for the chimp. Neither is the solution trivial to humans who watch the video. We can speculate that perhaps the solution was triggered when the chimp remembered that peanuts float or remembered the water in its cage or remembered that water raises some things. Perhaps, the memory of water's effect on peanuts (or some other things) was blended together with the perception of the peanut at the bottom of the tube to produce an internal image of the water being in the tube with the peanut on top. Perhaps, the blending never produced an internal image in the chimp but yet the blending allowed the chimp to know what to do. We will never know, but I wanted to experiment on myself to see if I could gain insight into what the chimp might have experienced.

MY EXPERIENCE WITHOUT LANGUAGE

First, I wanted to get rid of my language as much as possible so I could be more like the chimp. In Jill Bolte Taylor's book *My Stroke of Insight*, she described how during her stroke her language centers shut down and she entered an inner realm full of images. She described how it was so pleasant when her inner monologue was quieted. She entered a peaceful, more timeless existence where her inner voices that gave her constant reminders of today's agenda and constant evaluations of her work were absent. What peace, joy, and dazzling images were so near, but so far because of being a linguistic creature. I wanted to experience this type of inner world where images played a more significant role and language was quiet. However, I did not want to have a stroke!

So, I created a language-suppression technique. For a week during the summer, every time I noticed that I was thinking in language, I interrupted myself and forced myself to think in images and paused enough to feel how I was grounded in my body. During this week, I made sure that I had many outdoor activities to do at my house: mowing lawn, picking up brush in the woods on my property, and splitting wood. I wanted to be on the move doing tasks and solving problems as I walked about my yard and woods. I didn't want to be completely motionless like many of the meditation techniques I had tried in the past.

The first day (Monday) was mostly a day of constantly interrupting my inner dialogue. With a lifetime of being a language-user, the habit of maintaining an inner monologue was not going to go away easily. By the second day, I was doing much better. I started my language-suppression technique after my wife left for work. On the second day, when she returned from work she asked me a question and I only got around to answering her after a couple minutes. I heard her, but language seemed so far away now that I had entered a more embodied and image-rich existence. I now had to work to re-enter the world of language. Understandably, my wife did not like this long delay; so starting on the third day, I transitioned out of my image world about 45 minutes before she arrived home. By the time she got home, I was ready to speak in language again.

An amazing thing happened on the final day (Friday) of my experiment. I was splitting wood. To do so, I used a sledgehammer to pound a wedge into the wood until the wedge would stand by itself. I would have to hold the wedge upright with my left hand while I operated the sledgehammer with my right hand to pound on the top of the wedge. Then, when the wedge would stand, I grabbed the sledgehammer with both hands and pounded the wedge until it split the wood.

I noticed that my left hand was in danger of getting smashed when I was holding the wedge while I swung the sledgehammer with my right hand. I felt the danger, but I also formulated the problem in language in my mind: "There has to be a better way to drive the wedge so my left hand is not in danger." I noticed that I was thinking in language so I forced myself to think in images about the wedge, wood, and sledgehammer. Within three seconds of switching to images, an image of a solution popped fully formed into my mind. The *wedge stand* was born! (Figure 3.1).

Figure 3.1 The Wedge Stand. *Source*: The author owns the rights to this image and gives permission to Rowman & Littlefield to reprint it.

That weekend, I drew up a sketch of the invention and took it over to my next-door neighbor who happened to be a blacksmith for a historical village in the area. We agreed on a price for him to make what I had sketched. A week later, he delivered the new creation to my house. I rushed out to my wood pile to try it out. It worked just as I had imagined!

I knew that this was probably the closest I would ever get to understanding what it might be like to solve the peanut-in-the-tube problem as the chimpanzee did. For me, the invention came to me as a fully formed image. For the chimp, however, maybe no image was experienced. Perhaps, it just knew what actions to take without the use of an image. Again, we will never know. But that week of language suppression changed how I thought about how the mind works, how other mammals might solve problems, and how language relates to the rest of the mind.

TEMPLE GRANDIN'S EXPERIENCES

Reading Temple Grandin's books reaffirmed that my new views on how human minds relate to animal minds and how language fits into our inner world had some plausibility (Grandin, 2005, 2006). Temple Grandin is a PhD in animal science, who also is autistic. She communicates in language very well but says that it is not the way she thinks. She thinks in images. Two stories illustrate her way of thinking. First, if she hears the phrase, "church steeple," a whole series of steeples that she has experienced come into her mind. Her description reminds me of *Google Images*. Type in "church steeple" and an extensive array of actual church steeples appear. Temple claims that starting from the church steeples that she has experienced, she can manipulate the images to craft a steeple that she has never seen. She can alter an image based on color, material, shape, etc.

Further, Temple speculates that people with severe autism cannot engage in these editing processes. They are most likely confined by the church steeples they have actually experienced and cannot imagine a variation that combines features from several of them. In this way, these people could be described as trapped in the past (what they have experienced) and the present (what they are currently perceiving). According to her theory, they are very limited with regard to blending two memories (or a memory and a perception) to create something new.

People have a wide range of experiences. A good number of people do not image the many church steeples they have experienced when they hear the phrase "church steeple." They can remember particular steeples, if necessary, but they image more of a typical church steeple. Further, some may not be aware of any image in their minds when they follow the instructions to think of a church steeple. There are people who claim to never have an image in their minds. They can understand the sentence, "The church steeple was struck by lightning and part of it fell to the ground," and can make the proper deductions. The steeple might have fallen on a nearby street or into the church parking lot. There could be wind or rain damage on the inside of the church.

Their lack of awareness of an image, however, does not mean that their visual cortex is not active when understanding that sentence. It just means that the neural activity does not generate an experience of an image that comes into awareness. Perhaps, as for Jill Bolte Taylor, their language abilities dominate their inner experience and visual imagery consequently cannot rise to the level of awareness given the stiff competition. Brain scanning can help answer this question.

There are many possible individual differences among people. First, awareness of one's inner experience may be dominated by one type of information (e.g., linguistic) rather than another (e.g., visual). When a preferred type is interrupted, another can rise into awareness. Second, people will vary based on the level of detail they experience: highly detailed on one end of the spectrum and very abstract (e.g., the gist) on the other end. Third, they will differ based on their flexibility to blend things to make new fictional things. Some may stick closely to what they have experienced and others freely blend things so it seems to have little relation to what they have experienced.

AN ELK IN THE ROAD

Temple Grandin reports another inner experience that she says sheds light on how animals might think. Once, when she was driving an elk ran out in front of her car. Three images flashed into her mind: (1) the elk laying on her broken windshield, (2) the car behind her rear-ending her car, and (3) the elk passing safely across the road to the other side. Temple described these three images as possible outcomes based on how she responded. Attached to each image, so to speak, was a plan of action that her brain had worked out.

Temple remembers consciously choosing the most desirable image and her body knew what to do. If she did not brake at all, the elk would crash into her windshield. If she braked too hard, the car behind her would ram her car. If she braked just right, then the elk would pass safely in front of her car. She chose the image of the elk's safe passage and her foot pressed down on the brake the right amount.

Temple speculates that this might be the way that some higher animals might also solve problems. Their brains generate plans of action below the level of awareness. If multiple plans are generated, then multiple images come into awareness. The animal selects the most desirable image and the action plan is carried out. This general model is consistent with what is called a perception-action cycle. There is a repetitive cycle of first perceiving the world, second preparing a response, third executing an action as a response, and finally, perception restarts the cycle.

Joaquin Fuster (2004) illustrated this cycle as the movement of perceptual information upward into the organism until it is known what action to respond with. A reflex is the most automated response and the perceptual information does not go very far until a response action is executed. The farther the perceptual information goes upward in the cognitive system the less the being already has a habit ready to respond to it. We learn habits all the time. How to use a doorknob to open a door. How to use a pen to write. How to use a hammer, which is the philosopher Martin Heidegger's favorite example (Figure 3.2).

The more automatic these actions become, the less we have to think about them. If the perceptual information makes it all the way to the top, then there is no response ready to handle this perception. The matter of what to do is *unsettled*, as the American philosopher John Dewey likes to say. True thinking must then take place to plan what to do. We leave the world of being on auto-pilot and responding out of habit. We leave the world where matters are *settled*, in Dewey's terms. We enter the world where things are *unsettled*, where we need to truly think.

For example, suppose that a wall lamp is in an empty room and you need to unscrew the two flat-head screws to remove it from the wall. You do not want

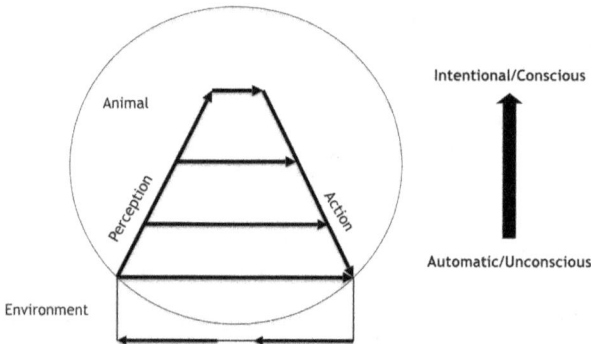

Figure 3.2 The Perception-Action Cycle. *Source*: The author drew this figure and gives permission to Rowman & Littlefield to reprint it.

to damage it or the wall. You have no screwdriver or other tools, other than what is on your person. How can you remove the lamp from the wall?

What makes this a problem is that everything you see has been *settled.* You learned that lamps are for giving off light, shades are for focusing the light, cords are for transporting electricity, plugs are for tapping into the electrical system. You have developed habits based on previous *inquiries,* as Dewey likes to say, where you learned what they are for and all these matters were *settled.* But now, these things are unsettled. You have to re-open the case of each of these closed inquiries.

Perhaps, the curve of the plastic lampshade could be used as a screwdriver. Better yet, perhaps the flat, rectangular prongs of the electric plug would make ideal screwdrivers. If these are too wide, then perhaps the button on your shirt, the pull of your zipper, the clasp of your belt or watch, the coin in your pocket, the credit card in your wallet, the earring or necklace of your jewelry, the nosepiece or earpiece of your glasses, or even your fingernail could be used as alternatives.

Habits close things over and settle the case of what a thing is for. Unsolved problems open up the closed cases and unsettle what was previously settled.

For example, suppose you come upon the following object that is unsettled for most people. What is it for? The only clue is that the wooden part is about two feet long. Since you do not know already, your brain has to truly think. Is the wooden part a handle of some sort? What does the metal end interact with? (Figure 3.3).

Basically, to understand the use of the mysterious object you have to imagine what it might be able to do and how you would operate it.

Maybe a dog catcher uses it to hook the collar of a dog while keeping the dog at a distance. Maybe train workers use it to snag hanging bags of mail while the train is moving. Maybe it is used to carry blocks of ice.

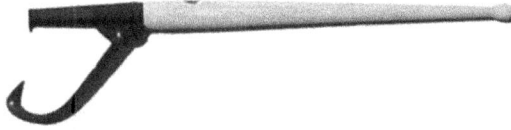

Figure 3.3   An Unfamiliar Object? *Source*: This tool is sold online by Labonville Inc. at http://www.labonville.com/Cant-Hook--Mill-Dog--173CH_p_495.html

No. It is called a *Cant Hook* and it is used to roll logs. The metal part grasps partly round a log and one person can get enough leverage from the handle to roll a heavy log all by themselves.

More than likely, in all these scenarios, your brain blended all the described elements together and simulated whether or not the use seemed plausible. Of course, some people are much better at creating accurate simulations than others.

SUMMARY

My experience of language-suppression, Jill Bolte Taylor's experience of a stroke, and Temple Grandin's experience of autism give us clues as to what our inner experience might be like without language and how language might relate to the rich inner world that exists without it. The next chapter (chapter 4) dives into the neuroscience and chapter 5 starts an extended discussion of how language could build upon the non-linguistic neural realm that precedes it.

REFERENCES

Bolte Taylor, J. (2009). *My stroke of insight: A brain scientist's personal journey.* New York: Penguin Books.

Fuster, J. M. (2004). Upper processing stages of the perception-action cycle. *TRENDS in Cognitive Science, 8,* 143–145.

Grandin, T. (2005). *Animals in translation.* New York: Scribner.

Grandin, T. (2006). *Thinking in pictures: My life with autism.* New York: Vintage Books.

Chapter 4

The Neuroscience behind Blending

(with Benjamin H. Zobel)

INTRODUCTION

In the thought experiment about the two mammals, we presented a simplified picture in which perceptions and memories are cleanly separated. The real situation is a bit more complicated.

As we will see, the mammalian brain is designed to handle the immediate future—that which will happen imminently. There is no debate on whether humans or any mammal can anticipate the immediate future. This ability seems to be built into the mammalian brain, as well as other animals. The immediate future is generally characterized as the next few hundred milliseconds.

The debate heats up among researchers, however, on whether any mammals besides humans can anticipate the non-immediate future. Some researchers refer to this as mental time travel into the future but mental time travel can also go into the non-immediate past. Can they anticipate what will happen in twenty minutes, in a day, in a week, in a month, in a year? To deal with the non-immediate future requires a collaboration between perception and memory that many mammals may be incapable of.

Michael Corballis, a prominent researcher in this area, stated back in 2007, along with his collaborator, Thomas Suddendorf, "there is as yet no convincing evidence for mental time travel in nonhuman animals" (Suddendorf and Corballis, 2007). However, he has softened his position in 2017 book (Corballis, 2017). There, he cites multiple examples, including the following.

A hungry chimpanzee comes upon a nut that is hard to crack. The chimp carries the nut some 80 meters to a place where days ago he had opened another nut with a piece of granite (Griffin, 2001). In 2012, a chimp in a zoo was reported to store away stones in a hidden place and then use them to throw at zoo visitors (Osvath and Karvonen, 2012). More generally, it has been reported that both chimps and bonobos can store away tools that experimenters gave them to help acquire food for up to fourteen hours before they need to use them. This behavior suggests that they were planning for the non-immediate future (Mulcahy and Call, 2006).

Presently, we will examine the neuroscience relevant to the immediate and non-immediate future.

THE PREDICTIVE BRAIN AND
THE IMMEDIATE FUTURE

Moshe Bar, in the introduction to his edited book, *The Proactive Brain* (Bar, 2011), states that the human brain "continuously generates predictions that anticipate the relevant future" (Bar, 2011: 13). Prior to the type of work collected in books such as Bar's, there was a great deal of focused research on retention/memory (the past) and attention (the present), but little on protention (the future). In the scientific literature, the study of how the brain deals with the future was scattered about under various names (e.g., priming, prediction, anticipation, expectation, prospection, pre-experience, pre-play, mental time travel, future thinking, and planning). After recent work, including Bar's, prediction has been promoted to equal status with memory and attention to become the trifecta of what the brain is constantly engaged in on a moment-to-moment basis.

This anticipatory neural activity is usually below our conscious awareness unless the prediction is wrong. Suppose a friend plays a trick on us. We ask our sneaky friend to get us a glass of Coke but they quietly return with a Dr. Pepper instead—which we also like. We reach for the glass. Our taste cortex (gustatory cortex) begins to fire in anticipation of an imminent Coke taste (Gazzaniga and colleagues, 2009). The taste of Dr. Pepper produces a neural activation pattern in the gustatory cortex which does not match the pattern that fired in expectation of the Coke. We experience surprise and a small bit of shock—even though we like Dr. Pepper. The expectation was not just at a high level of cognition in our frontal cortex ("I told my friend to get me a Coke and so I expect a Coke"). The expectation was also taking place at a lower level among the neural firings of our gustatory cortex.

In this way, our brain is continuously generating predictions that are either confirmed (sensory activation matches expectant activation) or denied in a sudden little surprise (sensory activation does not match expectant activation). The confirmed predictions usually stay below our awareness. The thwarted predictions, however, can rise up to the level of conscious awareness and are experienced as a bit of a shock.

NEURAL OVERLAP BETWEEN
MEMORY AND PREDICTION

Our brain is not a video camera that records what it experiences only to be retrieved exactly as it was experienced. It is now well established that memory is a reconstructive process (Bartlett, 1932; Friedman, 1993; Conway and Pleydell-Pearce, 2000; Hassabis and Maguire, 2007; Rubin and colleagues, 2003; Schacter and colleagues, 2007; Schacter and colleagues, 1998; Schacter and Addis, 2007). For this reason, our memories can be unreliable and can be manipulated to include things that are inaccurate.

Given that memory is a reconstructive process, neuroscientists have recently begun looking for differences in brain activity between remembering an event and imagining a future event that has not yet occurred. Strikingly, there is nearly a complete overlap in the brain areas that are activated for the two tasks (Botzung and colleagues, 2008; Okuda and colleagues, 2003; Szpunar and colleagues, 2007; Addis and colleagues, 2007). This finding suggests that the reconstruction of a past event and the construction of a hypothetical future event are very similar processes. Construction is crucial to both.

This intimate relationship between memory and future thinking is further supported by other types of evidence. People with extreme amnesia also cannot project themselves into possible future events—they are stuck in the present (Hassabis and colleagues, 2007; Klein and colleagues, 2002). Children develop the ability to remember past events and imagine future events at the same time (Suddendorf and Busby, 2003, 2005). The elderly decline in both abilities at the same time (Addis and colleagues, 2008).

THE REAL PURPOSE OF MEMORY:
PREPPING FOR THE FUTURE

"Why would humans, or any animal for that matter, have evolved a system that is at times quite unreliable? The answer is that there is no selective advantage to reconstructing the past *per se*, unless it matters for the present or future" (Suddendorf and Busby, 2003: 393). From an evolutionary standpoint focused on adaptability and survivability, the main job of our memories may be just to act as fodder for the effective assessment of future events (Suddendorf and colleagues, 2011; Suddendorf and Busby, 2003, 2005; Suddendorf and Corballis, 1997). The more we know the details of what has happened to us, the better we can devise the future events in our lives to make judgments of what to do in these possible situations. The real purpose of our memories is not so that humans can recount crimes we witnessed, contribute to a chronicle of historical events we lived through, or reminisce about the "good old days."

The main purpose is to help us construct detailed future scenarios so we can make decisions that benefit our survivability and that of our kin.

As we are poised in the present, it is evolutionarily more advantageous to lean toward the future than rest in the past. The past has already happened and we are still alive. The future is yet to happen and how we handle it will determine whether we live or die. Thus, in some sense, the future is more important than the past. Or, put another way, the past exists to serve the future, but not the other way around.

What kind of neural system is required to deal with the future? For one thing, it needs to be flexible. It can be constrained by the past, but not fully determined by it. "Since the future is not an exact replica of the past, simulation of future episodes may require a system that can draw on the past in a manner that flexibly extracts and recombines elements of previous experiences—a constructive rather than a reproductive system" (Schacter and Addis, 2007: 657).

If this constructive system were inflexible (i.e., too constrained by the past), it would not be able to waver from just recording events as they happened in the order they happened. The flexibility of this system, however, allows it not only to replay sequences of events in novel orders, but it can also fabricate events to some degree and pre-play these events that have never been experienced. This constructive process is just beginning to be understood, but researchers agree that there is some degree of randomness involved (i.e., stochastic neural activity) that can add to the novelty of what is constructed.

The implications of this constructive system are huge for many cognitive activities, including creative problem-solving. The flexibility of the construction system "permits the ability to 'manipulate' stored representations in the service of problem-solving behaviors" (Cohen and Eichenbaum, 1993). As Buckner (2010: 39) states, "This property, in an elaborated form, may have allowed our distant ancestors to evolve from primarily trial-and-error learners to mental explorers who solve problems by imagining the alternatives."

In order to assist in creative problem-solving behavior, the construction system needs to produce scenarios that are useful, partially accurate, actionable, and unified. For simplicity, we will call the neural activation pattern of a memory or a perception an image. By useful, we mean that it helps the mammal adapt and survive. In order to be useful, the constructed image needs to be partially accurate (i.e., similar to the current situation) but vary in important aspects so that the action plan based upon the constructed image would help solve the problem of the current situation. The constructed image needs to be associated with an actionable plan of response, meaning the mammal could actually carry it out. If the mammal imagines flying away from a predator, for example, the mammal cannot follow through on this fanciful image, unless the mammal were a bat or a flying squirrel.

Finally, a constructed image that is blended into a single image is more powerful for problem-solving than multiple images juxtaposed near each other. The next section uses an example to explain the power of a blended image over juxtaposed images.

THE POWER OF A BLENDED IMAGE

We will argue that being able to blend two images into one unified image is much more powerful than oscillating between multiple images. Any animal that can produce unified, blended images will have a distinct advantage in solving problems.

Consider the classic *Reverse Triangle Problem,* in which you need to find the fewest number of coins to move to get the triangle that is pointing upward on the left to point downward on the right.

In the side by side presentation in the top level of Figure 4.1, it usually takes people quite a while to try out many coin moves before they stumble upon the fewest number of coins. The eyes need to dart back and forth between the two patterns of coins.

However, if the starting and ending patterns are overlaid upon each other in a transparent manner so both can be seen at once as in the bottom level of Figure 4.1, then this problem becomes fairly easy. People can see directly that seven coins overlap and do not need to be moved, while three coins from each pattern are out of alignment. Just move three coins in the starting

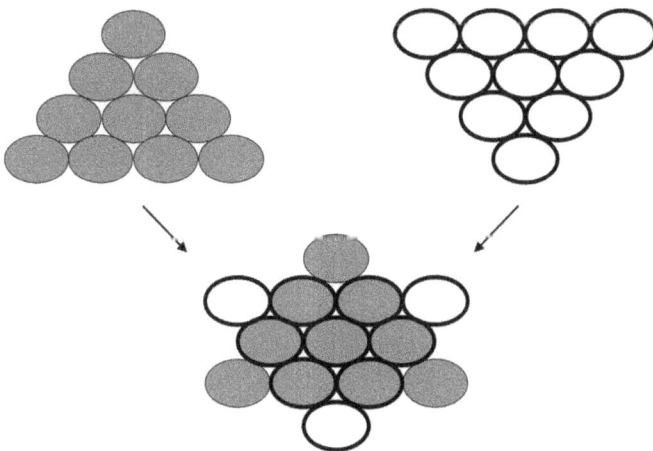

Figure 4.1 The Reverse Triangle Problem. *Source:* The author drew this figure and gives permission to Rowman & Littlefield to reprint it.

pattern and the ending pattern is achieved. Instead of alternating between two patterns, superimposition or proper blending permits direct perception of the final answer.

POSSIBILITIES OF NEURAL
EVOLUTIONARY MECHANISMS

What are possible neural changes that make blending possible? Neuroscientists will one day tell us in detail, but we present four hypotheses as candidate sources for consideration. First, blending perception and memory may become possible when the feedback connections in the visual system reach a certain ratio with respect to the number of feedforward connections. Currently, there are many more feedback connections than there are feedforward connections in the visual system (Gazzaniga and colleagues, 2009). Feedforward connections relate to processing what is perceived as the visual information moves forward through the visual cortex and beyond. Because the purpose of the feedback connections is not fully understood, our hypothesis is that one purpose is to help reinstate the neural states related to a visual memory. Thus, the feedforward connections deal with visual perception and may interact with the feedback connections dealing with visual memory. This place of interaction may be where blending takes place when concocting a fictional visual image that has actually never been experienced.

Already, there is substantial evidence that feedback pathways are involved in visual imagery (Miyashita, 1995) and their influence extends all the way to the earliest areas for processing visual perception (Kosslyn and colleagues, 2001). Further, much evidence shows that visual perception and visual imagery share many common processes (Farah, 1995; Ishai and Sagi, 1995; Miyashita, 1995). We leave it to vision researchers to test and further refine this hypothesis.

Second, the hippocampus plays a crucial role in the production of memories as well as their retrieval (i.e., reinstatement) (Gazzaniga and colleagues, 2009). The hippocampus has extensive connections throughout the cortex as memories are produced and later reinstated across the cortices related to our many senses. The hippocampus and its connections throughout the cortex together are sometimes called the hippocampal-cortical system (Buckner, 2010). Our second hypothesis is that the hippocampal-cortical system reached a critical number of cortical connections so that the retrieval of a memory (i.e., reinstatement of a perception) could have a significant influence on the activity associated with perception. In other words, this "tipping point" of cortical connections from the hippocampus permitted a true mixture of perception and memory to occur. Again, we will need neuroscientists to test and refine this hypothesis.

Third, when a human is not engaged in any particular task, certain brain networks called the *default-mode network* are still highly active. This activity is the default mode when no problem or task is pressing. This network is associated with daydreaming and thus would consist of fantasy, fiction, and speculating about the future. The hippocampus is among the many brain areas that are involved in this mind wandering network. The *default-mode network* is definitely identifiable in primates (Vincent and colleagues, 2007) and even in rats (Lu and colleagues, 2012). It is very possible that this network involves everything needed for blending and adding some control and guidance to the network permits it to do very useful work when problem-solving.

Fourth, in experiments with rats learning mazes, some scientists have used many implanted tiny electrodes that eavesdrop on neighboring neurons to understand what happens during the execution of the maze as well as sleeping after exploring the maze. Sometimes the neural firings while asleep duplicate the pattern of neural firings when the mouse was in the maze. In this way, the rat replays the maze in its sleep and this nocturnal activity is an important aspect of learning and remembering the maze.

However, the nocturnal activity may not always exactly duplicate the pathways that the rat actually engaged in while awake (Gupta and colleagues, 2010). Sleeping activation patterns may also present the reverse of the path that the rat actually traveled or even a path in a portion of the maze that the rat did not actually walk through. It is believed that this array of neural activity helps the rat develop an internal map of the maze—both the parts that it traveled and the neighboring parts that it did not (Derdikman and Moser, 2010). The flexibility of nocturnal replay points to the underlying pliability of our memories. This suppleness of memory replay and reconstruction most likely also serves the ability to produce fictions that are comprised of elements we have experienced.

SUMMARY

In our account, mammals initially relied on their sensorimotor systems that were designed to continuously plan actions for the immediate future based on what was being perceived. The onset of blending slightly altered this sensorimotor system so that the input to the sensorimotor system could also be a mixture of perception and memory rather than just perception alone. The relatively small neural changes necessary to allow blending caused a huge advance in ability. Mammals that could blend could devise and assess possible situations in order to make action plans for the non-immediate future. Before this step, mammals were basically stuck in the present and immediate future.

From here, mammals probably became gradually more skilled in intentionally initiating and controlling blends. The onset of language greatly increased the ability to control blends and initiate them in others.

In sum, the neural basis and evolutionary account of blending only add to its importance as a central tenet in cognitive science. The evolutionary neural account in this chapter shows what might have preceded blending and how non-linguistic animals may rely on blending during creative problem-solving. We look forward to neuroscientists fleshing out the details of how blending works, how blending came to be, and what intermediate steps preceded a form of blending that is under conscious control.

REFERENCES

Addis, D. R., Wong, A. T., & Schacter, D. L. (2007). Remembering the past and imagining the future: Common and distinct neural substrates during event construction and elaboration. *Neuropsychologia, 45,* 1363–1377.

Addis, D. R., Wong, A. T., & Schacter, D. L. (2008). Age-related changes in the episodic simulation of future events. *Psychological Science, 19,* 33–41.

Bar, M. (2011). The proactive brain. In M. Bar (Ed.), *Predictions in the brain* (pp. 13–26). Oxford University Press.

Bartlett, F. C. (1932). *Remembering: A study in experimental and social psychology.* Cambridge, England: Cambridge University Press.

Botzung, A., Denkova, E., & Manning, L. (2008). Experiencing past and future personal events: Functional neuroimaging evidence on the neural bases of mental time travel. *Brain and Cognition, 66,* 202–212.

Buckner, R. L. (2010). The role of the hippocampus in prediction and imagination. *Annual Review of Psychology, 62,* 27–48.

Cohen, N. J., & Eichenbaum, H. (1993). *Memory, amnesia, and the hippocampal system.* Cambridge, MA: MIT Press.

Conway, M. A., & Pleydell-Pearce, C. W. (2000). The construction of autobiographical memories in the self-memory system. *Psychological Review, 107,* 262–288.

Corballis, M. (2017). *The truth about language: What it is and where it came from.* Chicago, Illinois: University of Chicago Press.

Derdikman, D., & Moser, M. (2010). A dual role for hippocampal relay. *Science, 321,* 582–584.

Farah, J. M. (1995). The neural bases of mental imagery. In M. S. Gazzaniga (Ed.), *The cognitive neurosciences* (pp. 963–974). Cambridge, MA: MIT Press.

Friedman, W. J. (1993). Memory for the time of past events. *Psychological Bulletin, 113,* 44–66.

Gazzaniga, M. S., Ivry, R. B., & Mangun, G. R. (2009). *Cognitive neuroscience: The biology of the mind.* New York: Norton & Company.

Griffin, D. R. (2001). *Animal minds: From cognition to consciousness.* Chicago: University of Chicago Press.

Gupta, A. S., van de Meer, M. A., Touretzky, D. S., & Redish, A. D. (2010). Hippocampal replay is not a simple function of experience. *Neuron, 65,* 695–705.

Hassabis, D., Jumaran, D., Vann, S. D., & Maguire, E. A. (2007). Patients with hippocampal amnesia cannot imagine new experiences. *Proceedings of the National Academy of Sciences USA, 104,* 1726–1731.

Hassabis, D., & Maguire, E. A. (2007). Deconstructing episodic memory with construction. *Trends in Cognitive Science, 11,* 299–306.

Ishai, A., & Sagi, D. (1995). Common mechanisms of visual imagery and perception. *Science, 268,* 1772–1774.

Klein, S. B., Loftus, J., & Kihstrom, J. F. (2002). Memory and temporal experience: The effects of episodic memory loss on an amnesic patient's ability to remember the past and imagine the future. *Social Cognition, 20,* 353–379.

Kosslyn, S. M., Ganis, G., & Thompson, W. L. (2001). Neural foundations of imagery. *Nature Reviews Neuroscience, 2,* 635–642.

Lu, H., Zou, Q., Gu, H., Raichle, M., Stein, E., & Yang, Y. (2012). Rat brains also have a default mode network. *Proceedings of the National Academy of Sciences (USA), 109,* 3979–3984.

Miyashita, Y. (1995). How the brain creates imagery: Projection to primary visual cortex. *Science, 268,* 1719–1720.

Mulcahy, N. J., & Call, J. (2006). Apes save tools for future use. *Science, 312,* 1038–1040.

Okuda, J., Fujii, T., Ohtake, H., Tsukiura, T., Tanji, K. Suzuki, K., Kawashima, R., Fukuda, H., Itoh, M., & Yamadori, A. (2003). Thinking of the future and past: The roles of the frontal pole and the medial temporal lobes. *Neuroimage, 19,* 1369–1380.

Osvath, M., & Karvonen, E. (2012). Spontaneous innovation for future deception in a male chimpanzee, *Public Library of Science One (PLoS ONE), 7,* e36782.

Rubin, D. C., Schrauf, R. W., & Greenberg, D. L. (2003). Belief and recollection of autobiographical memories. *Memory and Cognition, 31,* 887–901.

Schacter, D. L., & Addis, D. R. (2007). The cognitive neuroscience of constructive memory: Remembering the past and imagining the future. *Philosophical Transactions of the Royal Society of London B: Biological Sciences, 362,* 773–786.

Schacter, D. L., Addis, D. R., & Buckner, R. L. (2007). Remembering the past to imagine the future: The prospective brain. *Nature Reviews Neuroscience, 8,* 657–661.

Schacter, D. L., Norman, K. A., & Koustaal, W. (1998). The cognitive neuroscience of constructive memory. *Annual Review of Psychology, 49,* 289–318.

Suddendorf, T., Addis, D. R., & Corballis, M. C. (2011). Mental time travel and the shaping of the human mind. In M. Bar (Ed.), *Predictions in the brain* (pp. 344–354). Oxford University Press.

Suddendorf, T., & Busby, J. (2003). Mental time travel in animals? *Trends in Cognitive Sciences, 7,* 391–396.

Suddendorf, T., & Busby, J. (2005). Making decisions with the future in mind: Developmental and comparative identification of mental time travel. *Learning and Motivation, 36,* 110–125.

Suddendorf, T., & Corballis, M. C. (1997). Mental time travel and the evolution of the human mind. *Genetic, Social and General Psychology Monographs, 123,* 133–167.

Suddendorf, T., & Corballis, M. C. (2007). The evolution of foresight: What is mental time travel, and is it unique to humans? *Behavioral and Brain Sciences, 30,* 299–351.

Szpunar, K. K., Watson, J. M., & McDermott, K. B. (2007). Neural substrates of envisioning the future. *Proceedings of the National Academy of Sciences USA, 104,* 642–647.

Vincent, J., Patel, G., Fox, M., Snyder, A., Baker, J., Van Essen, D., Zempel, J, Snyder, L., Corbetta, M., & Raichle, M. (2007). Intrinsic function architecture in the anesthetized monkey brain. *Nature, 447,* 83–86.

Chapter 5

Language's Relation to Other Cognitive Abilities

INTRODUCTION

In this and the next two chapters, we will examine human linguistic abilities in a way that will lead to ways to analyze and diagnose comprehension issues that students may be experiencing. Here is an overview. Babies have significant cognitive abilities before they acquire language. Language is built upon these cognitive abilities. Language has various relations with our diverse pre-linguistic abilities. Language may integrate nicely with some, amplify others, provide short-cuts to access others, and in some cases make possible new cognitive abilities. However, language can also mask over some of our cognitive abilities making them harder to notice.

A branch of linguistics called *Cognitive Linguistics* focuses on how language is built upon these underlying pre-linguistic abilities. Some of these linguists conceive of grammar as a loose set of instructions for building up an inner simulation of the events and relationships presented in a description. Some students' problems with language comprehension could partly come from their struggle to transform from a grammatical form to an inner simulation. Some of their writing problems could partly be a struggle to transform their inner mental simulation into a linear set of grammatical forms.

One approach to access our inner way of building up simulations is to use a film director's jargon (e.g., cut, zoom in, pan left) to see how each visual command corresponds to grammatical forms. An inability to cognitively perform one of these camera maneuvers may result in being unable to understand text that triggers that maneuver during the creation of an internal simulation. This is one way that grammar and text can be analyzed in terms of the underlying cognitive operations that are involved in the making of meaning.

BEFORE A BABY ACQUIRES LANGUAGE

A great deal happens with our brains before a person acquires language. The brain is constructed in the womb. The neurons are created and placed into position. The brain starts processing at least auditory, tactile, and proprioceptive information before birth. The brain starts processing lighted, visual information after birth. Even before birth, an initial, tentative profile of cognitive strengths and weaknesses may emerge among various modalities that are beginning to cooperate with each other. This profile is further adjusted once the child is born and visual information is fully added into the mix. So much takes place before a child utters his/her first word.

As language is acquired, it upsets the balance of the processing modes that existed before it. Maybe a better way to state this: language acquisition reorganizes the brain and how the previously established modalities relate to each other. As described in more detail in the next chapter, each word triggers activity all across the cerebral cortex depending on the various meanings of the word and the modalities involved. For example, the word *top* simultaneously activates the same area where other words for clothing items also induce activity, an area for spatial information, and an area for buildings and places. Further, the word *chair* would trigger brain areas related to the processing of various modalities: visual, tactile (texture), motor (how to sit in a chair and how to get up out of it), possibly sound (for experiences of squeaky chairs), other words, and possibly other modalities.

In this way, language—first as an auditory experience and later as a visual experience—establishes linkages across the cerebral cortex that are activated first for a sound pattern of a word and then for a visual pattern of a word. This condensed way of triggering coordinated neural activity across the brain is an amazing feat. The effects for us as individuals and for us as a species are truly astounding. We can trigger amazing neural patterns in our fellow language speakers with just a short sequence of sounds or a few marks on a paper. We do not have to carry the relevant objects around in our hands or act out the events with our bodies. We can spark experiences in others that have never happened before or that are even impossible to exist with nothing more than a few sounds or a few marks on paper.

SOME DOWNSIDES TO LANGUAGE

Importantly, we must remember that language is built upon a set of pre-existing brain systems that are already highly coordinated and orchestrated. We can remember actual objects/events and imagine yet-to-exist objects/events before language was ever present either for our species or for each of us as individuals. Interestingly, what happens within an individual's development repeats what happened at the species level before humans possessed language. In traditional terms, ontogeny recapitulates phylogeny.

The benefits of language are astoundingly clear and have been written about extensively. However, there may be a few disadvantages to acquiring language, especially for the individual.

In some cases, language comes to dominate our experience in that its absence reveals a rich inner life that language masked. As discussed in a previous chapter, Jill Bolte Taylor, in her book *My Stroke of Insight*, reports how a rich, inner life of images came forth into her awareness during and after a stroke that quieted her language abilities. My language-suppression technique allowed me to visually invent the *wedge stand* in a matter of seconds and permitted me to experience a depth of awareness of color, touch, and empathy that I had never experienced before. Language's place in a person's inner profile of modalities may dominate their awareness and force other types of processing to sink beneath their level of awareness.

Some stroke victims discover or alter their ability to draw, paint, or sculpt. The strokes do not have to be near the normal language areas of Broca's and Wernicke's areas, but they often are. For example, after a stroke, a 54-year-old man who was a house builder suddenly became a talented poet, painter, and sculptor—activities that he showed no interest in before the stroke (Treffert, 2011). Dementia in the frontotemporal areas most often influences both the front and temporal lobes and typically affects language, decision making, executive control, and emotions. Miller and colleagues (1996, 1998) described five people who became talented realistic painters only after the onset of frontotemporal dementia. The scientists hypothesized that the people had greater access to information from their visual systems which allowed all of them to paint in a highly detailed realistic fashion but did not allow them to paint in an abstract style. Further, the temporal damage was on the left side which would contribute to the decreased influence of language abilities.

Dr. Darold Treffert is considered the foremost authority on how surprising abilities can arise in people after stroke, focal dementia, or a traumatic impact to the brain. He has two books filled with detailed case studies on a wide variety of triggers of special talent (Treffert, 2011, 2013). In the cases of brain trauma, the brain changes may have caused a reorganization to produce new abilities that were not present before. There is the distinction, however, between unleashing abilities that were there all the time and producing new abilities. The line between them is probably quite subtle.

There is even evidence that low-level electrical stimulation of the left frontotemporal region can improve artistic ability, proofreading skills, and accurately guessing the number of items when a fairly large number are shown. Allan Snyder has done much of this work and argues that interfering with the left frontotemporal area inhibits their function which gives us access to less processed, non-linguistic information that is usually below the level of awareness (Snyder, 2009).

Usually, most of us live at a level where small details of visual information, for example, are subsumed under the gist of what we see as we categorize it for its overall meaning. Once we are aware of this lower level of detail, however, we can possibly improve our drawing ability, attention to the details of spelling, or assessing the number of items set in front of us.

This basic process seems to partly explain the abilities we encounter in natural savants, who always seemed to have a heightened ability; and acquired savants, who develop exceptional abilities after disease or a traumatic event to the brain. However, it is not always the left frontotemporal that is initially affected. A stroke in the visual area of the brain significantly altered the art style of one painter to a more abstract style (Treffert, 2013). The thought is that the stroke interfered with access to small visual details.

PRE-LINGUISTIC ABILITIES INFLUENCE LANGUAGE ACQUISITION

By the time children acquire their first words, they have already secured a great deal of sensory and motor information about their world (Bloom, 2000; Langer, 2001). In fact, much of their hand and finger movements are the result of intensive coordination between the visual and motor systems of the brain. More specifically, the brain uses signals from the two eyes to develop a three-dimensional model of the world. The reaching action of the hands for an object gradually becomes more accurate in its positioning and timing within the 3D world.

All of the sensorimotor expertise greatly informs the order of what words are acquired first (Mandler, 1992; Smith and Jones, 1993). Children naturally learn the names of objects and actions that they have the most experience with. More generally, the more easily a word can be imaged, the earlier it is learned (Gillette and colleagues, 1999). Further, more nouns than verbs are learned earlier (Gentner, 1982).

After learning just 50 words, most of them probably nouns, a child's behavior shows an attunement to some strategies to learn new words. In English, new nouns are often introduced to young children using a consistent grammar form such as "This is a _____" (Smith, 1999). The sentence is combined with either holding the object, pointing to it or joint attention toward it. Also, adjectives can be introduced with a constant grammar form such as "This *noun* is _____" or "_____ *noun*" (Smith, 1999).

Around the acquisition of 300 words, children begin to be able to put words together when they express themselves (Bates and Goodman, 1999). At around 28 months of age, children generally begin to quickly acquire many new ways to put words together.

Older children learn new words at such a fast rate that they cannot physically encounter each referent of all these new words (Bloom, 2000). They need to learn new words through their relations with other words. For example, descriptions of new concrete nouns can be learned based on known concrete nouns: "A zebra is somewhat like a horse but it is black with white stripes." Or, descriptions of abstract nouns can be based on already known words: "Envy is a feeling which may occur when you really want something that someone else has."

We can greatly increase our vocabularies by scaffolding our way up this abstract word hierarchy using only words to learn other words. A dictionary is a place where words are defined almost exclusively by other words—however, there is an occasional image. It is a closed system, so to speak, in that, if you left out the rare pictures that occurred, each word points to other words to elucidate its meaning. It is a world of words and only words. It takes a human that has a certain minimal vocabulary to use a dictionary in an effective manner. If a person only knew a few words, then when reading a definition of a new word, they would have to look up most of the words they encounter. Not only would this be time-consuming, but at some level, it would also be highly ineffective.

If you only knew ten words, for example, could you start to use a dictionary? If you knew what the word "horse" refers to, how many words would you need to know to get the basic idea of a zebra? In the "definition" of *zebra* above, twelve different words were used to characterize *zebra:* "A zebra is somewhat like a horse but it is black with white stripes." Some words were repeated. Remember no pictures are allowed in our little thought experiment.

So, a person would have to know about twelve words to get some sense of what a zebra is. Still, we would not know much about it. We would just know its basic shape and color scheme. And, we would have had to, at least, have seen a picture of a horse to ground our understanding. Knowing the word *horse* and having seen a picture (or a drawing) would seem to be sufficient for us to image a zebra. Maybe not very accurately, but we are exploring the minimum experiential requirements necessary. Of course, we would have to know what a *stripe* is and the colors black and white. And, if we knew black and white, we probably have experienced other colors and may even know their names.

Without some experience with our sense modalities, can any words have meaning? Children learn language from the concrete upward. They have to have sense experience to ground and bootstrap the whole process of language acquisition (Howell and colleagues, 2005). Along with some amount of sense experience, they also need to be able to blend things together. They need to conjure up black and white stripes and put them on the shape of a horse. So, there is an amazing amount going on to move from the experience of *horse, black, white*, and *stripe* in order to combine it into something coherent so we can say that we understand in a minimal way what the word *zebra* refers to.

UNDERSTANDING A LANGUAGE WITHOUT ANY EXPERIENCE?

The philosopher John Searle created a thought experiment in which he imagined a monolingual English-speaking person locked in a room who has access to manuals telling her in English how to transform sequences of Mandarin Chinese symbols into other sequences of Mandarin Chinese. Each sequence of symbols is written on paper and slid under the door. She then follows her manuals, writes down a new sequence, and slides the new piece of paper back under the door. The manuals are so good and the person in the room becomes so proficient at this task that people outside the door are convinced that the person in the room is fluent in Mandarin Chinese. She is carrying out a nice conversation in Chinese with the people outside of the room (Searle, 1980).

In fact, the person in the room is just following instructions and does not know any Chinese. Given this set-up, Searle argues that by analogy a computer that just manipulates symbols cannot be said to understand a language. It is just blindly following rules. The symbols the human is working with are not grounded in any sense experience for her that refers to something out in the world. The person is fluent in English but does not know the meaning of even one symbol of Mandarin Chinese.

Some have argued that although the person does not know Chinese, the combination of the person and all the translation manuals know Chinese. Others are convinced by Searle's argument that the meaning of a language must be grounded in the level of sense experience which exists outside of the symbols. Children's acquisition of language builds upon words that are highly "sensible" and proceeds up to more abstract words that are only indirectly grounded in sensible experience.

MONKEYS UNDERSTANDING ABSTRACT WORDS?

Determining which words are abstract and which are concrete, however, can be a bit tricky. In a classic and funny experiment, scientists tried to determine whether capuchins monkeys understood the concepts of "fairness" and "justice." Many philosophers have discussed these ideas and it seemed they involved an abstract weighing of often many factors of a situation.

The experimenters gave a first capuchin monkey a cucumber slice. Capuchins generally like cucumber and the first capuchin gladly ate it. However, then the experimenter gave the second capuchin a grape in the sight of the first capuchin. Capuchins like grapes much more than cucumber slices. Finally, the experimenter gave the first capuchin a cucumber slice, who threw it back and hit the experimenter.

People laugh and laugh at this video (https://www.youtube.com/watch?v=gOtlN4pNArk). Cucumber slices were acceptable until something better was offered to a neighbor. The reaction of throwing the cucumber slice at the experimenter rings true in a comical way that "fairness" is not a very abstract concept but can be easily grounded in experience. Young children easily exclaim "That's not fair," but it is even more striking to see a capuchin monkey embody a sense of unfairness.

This is just one of many fairness experiments done with primates and their videos are fun to watch. The full notion of *justice* may still be more abstract than this example with cucumbers and grapes because can it can deal with cases in which someone murdered another person. You cannot bring the person back to life, so how can justice be served? Should the murderer be killed, have their freedom taken away for life, or have their freedom taken away for a certain number of years? What is just in this case? Philosophers and judges still have much room to weigh and debate the more abstract cases of fairness and justice.

COMPUTER TRANSLATION AND "UNDERSTANDING"

In any case, an incredible amount of information can be gleaned from just analyzing how often some words co-occur with other words. Landauer and Dumais (1997) created a statistical process called Latent Semantic Analysis (LSA) that processed large quantities of text to determine what contexts certain words appeared in. For example, the word *top* could occur with other words for toy, words for clothing, and words for spatial relationships. These are some of the contexts that *top* appears in. When LSA has analyzed huge amounts of written text, its behavior matched human behavior on certain tasks: vocabulary tests, sorting words into various categories, and association tests (what words come to mind when you hear a particular word), to name a few (Landaur, Laham, and Foltz, 1998). So, some aspects of human knowledge can be quite accurately modeled just by staying within the closed system of words relating to other words and never venturing out into human sensory experience.

Further, *Google Translate* initially used a statistical approach that analyzed the co-occurrence of words across large amounts of text that had already been translated from one language to another. In late 2016, *Google Translate* switched to a deep neural network model to determine the equivalencies between sentences in each language.

In sum, there is no doubt that an incredible amount of information can be extracted from just examining how words relate to words with no grounding in sense experience: dictionaries, grammar books, data on which words co-occur with other words, and data on which words in one language are often used to translate which words in another language. But all this symbol comparison and manipulation would ultimately have no meaning if there were no humans around that used the languages involved.

A human brings the text alive, so to speak, by constructing a coherent set of neural activity patterns that correspond to something the person can either experience or imagine. Without the human as an organism that understands, the computations performed on text created are just an exercise in mathematics and symbol manipulation. In my opinion, these computations provide a great service to humans but are not ultimately "symbols come alive," so to speak, but stay at the level of "dead operations on symbols."

BASIC GRAMMAR TRIGGERS MENTAL SIMULATIONS

Humans have a rich inner life that is comprised of so many simultaneous neural activities: visual, auditory, tactile, taste, smell, linguistic, emotions, memories, daydreams, to name a few. When we express something from our internal world with a verbal language, we drastically reduce it to a linear stream of sounds that then triggers the construction of another collection of neural activities in others who understand the same language.

Any linear expression such as *red pencil* (an example used by Fauconnier and Turner, 2002) can trigger the onset of multiple neural activities. The neural activity might correspond to a pencil with red lead, a red shaft, both red lead and a red shaft. Further, the neural pattern might correspond to a pencil that is used to record debits (i.e., in the red financially), a Communist pencil, a yellow-shafted pencil with a streak of red paint on it that distinguishes it from the other yellow-shafted pencils, a pencil used by a bleeding person, a pencil used by a red-headed person, etc. Perhaps, the neural activity for many or all of these is initially triggered, but the context narrows down things so that one of the neural patterns wins—so to speak.

The brain is often exorbitant in all the neural activity it initially unleashes, but then one of the options usually wins. This is not just true for language comprehension but for our motor actions. The brain usually devises several action plans in response to stimuli and the basal ganglia helps choose which plan "wins" and is actually carried out.

For *red pencil*, one of the neural patterns probably fits better with the overall neural pattern that has been built up based on other information and it wins—or endures when the others fade. If multiple neural patterns for *red pencil* fit in with the overall neural pattern, then the situation is ambiguous. In this case, multiple patterns for *red pencil* stay alive and the person will need further information to select one.

Notice that I have been avoiding the word *meaning* for the phrase *red pencil* and the word *context* for the build-up of neural activity based on the past, present, and anticipated future. I wanted to emphasize the neural grounding of these common terms. Deep down, it all grounds itself in neural patterns of activity.

THE GRAMMATICAL FORM NOUN-NOUN

Red pencil follows a simple grammatical form *adjective-noun*. Let us now consider the form *noun-noun*. Imagine what *steak puddle* might mean. These two nouns and their accompanying neural profiles may have never been activated simultaneously before. What might the two activation patterns blend into as they unify? Or, will they unify at all? If they unify, then we have made sense of them. If not, then we are left with nonsense. Notice that the term *nonsense* implies that the simultaneously active neural patterns have not blended into a neural pattern that grounds to something we can sense as one thing. It does not gel into something that is sensible. This way of understanding the terms *sense* and *nonsense* highlights the fact that our neural profile is grounded in so many modalities, many of them related to our senses, and *making sense* means constructing something that ultimately is unified and ultimately grounds in our senses.

What sense can you make of *steak puddle*? It could be a puddle where you throw the bad steaks. It could be the puddle that forms when a frozen steak thaws out. It could be the puddle of drool that forms when a person salivates over a steak. It could be what emerges from a blender after you use it on a steak—so people requiring soft food can eat it. It could be many other things.

Notice that we had to create a scenario in which we borrowed aspects of the neural activation of *steak* and the neural activation of *puddle* and then unified them into something that we could then refer to. We took a multiplicity and created a unity. The philosopher Alfred North Whitehead describes creativity as "The many become one and are increased by one" (Whitehead, 1929). He means that to create something you need to unify a multiplicity. Once you do, then the new unity becomes a new member of the multiplicity and increases the size of the set of the multiplicity by one member.

In my research, I crafted a computer program that randomly generated noun-noun combinations from Princeton's extensive online thesaurus *Word-Net* (Miller, 1995). Amazingly, if a person understood the two nouns then they could make sense of the combination. We never found a counterexample that remained nonsensical for very long. We humans are generally pretty awesome when it comes to making sense of apparent nonsense.

Some cognitive psychologists have attempted to articulate the various relations that could be used to unify any two nouns. The number of relations ranges from 12 (Levi, 1978) to 30 (Nastase and Szpakowicz, 2003). No category scheme is perfect, but here is the most extensive set of categories (Nastase and Szpakowicz, 2003; O'Seaghdha, 2008).

Causality

Flu virus, virus CAUSES flu
Math anxiety, anxiety is the EFFECT of math
Concert hall, concerts are the PURPOSE of the hall
Headache pill, a pill DETRACTS from a pain of a headache

Quality

Hat box, a box CONTAINS a hat
Carrot cake, cake CONTENTS include carrots
Player coach, a particular player IS BOTH (EQUALS) the coach
Brick house, house is made from the MATERIAL brick
Saturation point, this point MEASURES the complete saturation
Weather report, the weather is the TOPIC of the report
Oak tree, this tree is of TYPE oak

Temporality

Daily exercise, exercise is done at a daily FREQUENCY
Morning exercise, exercise takes place in the morning (TIME AT)
Six-hour meeting, the meeting lasted six hours (TIME THROUGH)

Participant

Student protest, the students were the AGENTS of the protest
Student discount, the student is the BENEFICIARY of the discounts
Laser printer, the laser is the INSTRUMENT of the printing

Metal separator, the separator separates metal (OBJECT)
Sunken ship, being sunken is the PROPERTY of the OBJECT ship (OBJECT PROPERTY)
Printer tray, the printer tray is a PART of the printer
Group plan, the group is the POSSESSOR of the plan
Plum tree, the tree makes the PRODUCT plums
Novelty item, being novel is a PROPERTY of the item
Olive oil, olives are the SOURCE of the oil
Cell division, cell division names a new STATE (STATIVE)
Daisy chain, a daisy chain is a WHOLE made of many parts.

Spatial

Exit route, exit route names a DIRECTION for this route
Home town, the LOCATION of the town
Desert storm, the storm is LOCATED in the desert, (LOCATION AT)
Country butter, the butter comes from the countryside (LOCATION FROM)

These sets of relations describe the key connection required to unify the two nouns. For *headache pill,* for example, it might be a pill that prevents a headache, a pill that relieves a headache, a pill that causes a headache—among other things. Even after using these longer phrases to explain the noun-noun combo in more detail; still, you ultimately have to ground the language in a collection of coherent neural activities that focus on a particular way that *headaches* and *pills* can blend into one thing. The end of the process is not a long description of many words that details what the noun-noun combo refers to. That is not the meaning of *steak puddle.* Ultimately, to understand something a mind has to be able to *image* something. Not *image* in the sense of just visual information. A better way to say it: to understand something, the neural activity for each element must blend into one coherent activity pattern so that all the modes of neural activity coalesce and support the presentation of the same *thing.*

SUMMARY

Many cognitive abilities are developed to some degree before a young human acquires his/her first words. We are generally well aware of the many benefits of language, but having a language also comes with a cost. Our linguistic ability may come to dominate our awareness and hide some non-linguistic abilities from us. Events such as stroke, dementia, and brain trauma may unleash abilities that we already had but were unaware of or cause new abilities to form—or maybe, a bit of both.

Language is built upon our non-linguistic abilities and influences the order in which we learn various linguistic components. Although computers can extract much useful information from just analyzing large amounts of text; ultimately the meanings of short phrases such as *red pencil* and *steak puddle* are what is experienced when the neural activations of both words coalesce into a coherent neural pattern that presents a unified thing. In short, no brain, no meaning.

The next chapter will examine larger grammatical constructs and how a film director's language (zoom, pan, etc.) can help describe the mental operations involved as people understand larger quantities of text.

REFERENCES

Bates, E., & Goodman, J. C. (1999). On the emergence of grammar from the lexicon. In B. MacWhinney (Ed.), *The emergence of language*. New Jersey: Lawrence Erlbaum Associates.

Bloom, P. (2000). *How children learn the meaning of words*. Cambridge: Cambridge University Press.

Bolte Taylor, J. (2009). *My stroke of insight: A brain scientist's personal journey*. New York: Penguin Books.

Fauconnier, G., & Turner, M. (2002). *The way we think: Conceptual blending and the mind's hidden complexities*. Basic Books.

Gentner, D. (1982). Why nouns are learned before verbs: Linguistic relativity versus natural partitioning. In S. Kuczaj (Ed.), *Language development, Vol. 2: Language, thought, and culture* (pp. 301–334). Hillsdale, NJ: Lawrence Erlbaum.

Gillette, J., Gleitman, H., Gleitman, L., & Lederer, A. (1999). Human simulations of vocabulary learning. *Cognition, 73*, 135–176.

Howell, S. R., Jankowicz, D., & Becker, S. (2005). A model of grounded language acquisition: Sensorimotor features improve lexical and grammatical learning. *Journal of Memory and Language, 53*, 258–276.

Landauer, T. K., & Dumais, S. T. (1997). A solution to Plato's problem: The latent semantic analysis theory of the acquisition, induction, and representation of knowledge. *Psychological Review, 104*, 211–242.

Landauer, T. K., Laham, D., & Foltz, P. (1998). *Learning human-like knowledge by singular value decomposition: A progress report*.

Langer, J. (2001). The mosaic evolution of cognitive and linguistic ontogeny. In M. Bowerman & S. C. Levinson (Eds.), *Language acquisition and conceptual development*. Cambridge: Cambridge University Press.

Levi, J. N. (1978). *The syntax and semantics of complex nominals*. New York and San Francisco: Academic Press.

Mandler, J. M. (1992). How to build a baby: II. Conceptual primitives. *Psychological Review, 99*, 587–604.

Miller, G. (1995). WordNet: A lexical database for English. *Communications of the ACM, 38(11),* 39–41.

Miller, B. L., Cummings, J., Mishkin, F., Boone, K., Prince, F., Ponton, M., & Cotman, C. (1998). Emergence of artistic talent in frontotemporal dementia. *Neurology, 51(4).* DOI: https://doi.org/10.1212/WNL.51.4.978

Miller, B. L., Ponton, M., Benson, D. F., Cummings, J. L., & Mena, I. (1996). Enhanced artistic creativity with temporal lobe degeneration. *Lancet, 348(9043),* 1744–1745. DOI: https://doi.org/10.1016/S0140-6736(05)65881-3

Nastase, V., & Szpakowicz, S. (2003). Exploring noun-modifier semantic relations. In *Proceedings of the 5th International Workshop on Computational Semantics (IWCS-03).* Tilburg: The Netherlands.

O'Seaghdha, D. (2008). Learning compound noun semantics. Technical Report #735 (UCAM-CL-TR-735, ISSN 1476-2986), University of Cambridge Computer Laboratory.

Searle, J. (1980). Minds, brains, and programs. *Behavioral and Brain Sciences, 3,* 417–424.

Smith, L. B. (1999). Children's noun learning: How general learning processes make specialized learning mechanisms. In B. MacWhinney (Ed.), *The emergence of language.* New Jersey: Lawrence Erlbaum Associates.

Smith, L. B., & Jones, S. S. (1993). The place of perception is children's concepts. *Cognitive Development, 8(2),* 113–139.

Snyder, A. (2009). Explaining and inducing savant skills: Privileged access to lower level, less-processed information. *Philosophical Transactions of the Royal Society of London. Series B, Biological Sciences, 364,* 1399–1405.

Treffert, D. (2011). *Islands of genius: The bountiful mind of the autistic, acquired, and sudden savant.* Philadelphia, PA: Jessica Kingsley Publishers.

Treffert, D. (2013). *The 'Acquired' Savant—'Accidental' genius: Could such dormant potential exist within us all?* https://www.wisconsinmedicalsociety.org/profe ssional/savant-syndrome/resources/articles/the-acquired-savant-accidental-genius/

Whitehead, A. N. (1929). *Process and reality.* New York: Macmillan Company.

Chapter 6

Transforming Language
to Neural Activity

INTRODUCTION

For simplicity, we will divide linguists into two types. First, there are follow-ers of Noam Chomsky's approach. They focus on the structure of the lan-guage that humans produce. They even look for universals that apply to any possible human language. Second, there are *Cognitive Linguists* that focus on the cognitive and neural operations underlying the production and com-prehension of language. In particular, they tend to view language as just one manifestation of meaning construction that goes on in the neural background at all levels of brain processing. Understanding a visual scene is another form of meaning construction.

As Gilles Fauconnier says of this approach that ties together linguistics and cognition, "A deep result of the research is the fact that the same prin-ciples operate at the highest levels of scientific, artistic, and literary thought as do the lower levels of elementary understanding and sentence meaning" (Fauconnier, 1997). In this approach, meaning making is the operative goal in every modality and level of brain organization. Language is just one of the modes where meaning construction happens and it requires the integra-tion of many modalities to reach a unified interpretation of the grammati-cal text.

The grammatical text does not have meaning in and of itself, but rather has the potential for meaning (Fauconnier, 1997). The words and grammar trigger the meaning construction processes all throughout the brain. The final product of a sentence might be a simulation that emulates the basics of a scene. Your brain is reenacting an event in a muted fashion when compared to the neural activation from actually experiencing the described scene.

Or, the final product might be a simulation of the relationships that hold in a math expression or in a line of computer code.

BRAIN ATLAS OF WHERE WORDS ACTIVATE

Neuroscientists mapped what brain areas were active when people listened to a story (Huth and colleagues, 2016). They found individual differences, but also a general pattern that the same word generally activated similar regions based on its possible meanings. For example, the word *top* activated an area where other clothing words also triggered activation, another area related to numbers and spatial relations, and another area related to buildings and places. Prior to studies like this, researchers had focused on the location of language to the areas related to speech production, Broca's area, and language comprehension, Wernicke's area.

The present study showed that pretty much the entire cortex was involved in language comprehension. This study is consistent with the emerging view that language comprehension is based on creating a mental simulation of the scene that is being described to you. Concrete words, such as chair, will trigger the visual areas of the brain as it is integrated into a narrative scene—as well as other areas. A chalkboard will trigger visual information and possibly auditory information from the squeak of chalk upon it, as well as smell information and touch information for the smell and texture of chalk dust. The emerging view is that comprehension involves recreating the described scene as if you were experiencing it. The experience of recreating a described scene is generally muted compared to an actual experience, unless it triggers a traumatic event associated with PTSD (post-traumatic stress disorder), for example.

NEURAL PROFILES

One way to visualize both the wealth of neural activity and individual differences related to each word is through the graph in Figure 6.1. Imagine the assorted neural activity for a chair. There would probably be a great deal of visual activity and motor activity for how to sit down in a chair. Further, there would usually not be much activity related to smell or taste.

Certainly, the bars of the graph could differ greatly based on individual differences. Of course, a person blind from birth would have no visual activity. An acrobat who uses chairs to balance on might have much more motor activity than others. A person highly attuned to color would have a certain type of visual information highlighted. The list of possible individual differences goes on and on.

Profile of the Neural Activity for a Chair

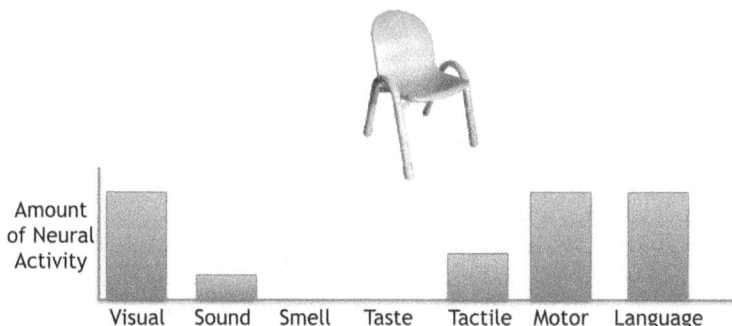

Figure 6.1 Neural Profile of a Chair. *Source*: The author drew this figure and gives permission to Rowman & Littlefield to reprint it.

AHA MOMENTS AND UNI MOMENTS

A masterful teacher might bring forth apparently disconnected elements to a story and then finally connect it all together at the end of class so that the students have an *aha moment*—a sudden revelation of insight. Or, a masterful teacher might make each point of a complex topic understandable so that students can easily follow every move. It is not until class is over that the students realize that they now understand key aspects of a difficult topic such as quantum mechanics, for example.

The first way of proceeding produces an *aha moment* and important work by neuroscientists John Kounious and Mark Beeman (2015) have detailed the neural underpinnings of how these sudden moments of insight occur in the brain and how they rise into awareness.

The second way of proceeding produces what I am calling a *uni moment,* which is short for a unification moment or a moment of unity. In the case described with the masterful teacher, the "moment" lasts basically the entire class period. Or, more accurately, there is a series of the *uni moments* as the teacher introduced a new idea and then quickly integrates it into the story of the presentation. Because these "moments" are low key, students would not generally describe them as a series of sudden insights (or *aha moments*). Instead, these moments seem more fluid and naturally integrated into what came before. There may be a continuity of spectrum between *uni moments* and *aha moments*, with different students disagreeing on which one they experienced at which time. In other words, these two differ by degree and there are individual differences as to when people would report which one.

Neuroscientists have yet to really focus on these more subtle moments— these quiet cousins of *aha moments*. However, there are topics in the neuroscience literature that point to the underlying idea. Some neuroscience research focuses on synchronous behavior among the neural activity of sometimes distant parts of the brain. Others use the term *coherence* to describe an alignment among various areas of neural activity. The basic idea is that in some way a coherent idea is matched by "coherent" neural activity. In other words, neuroscientists are looking for some neural signature that distinguishes between encountering something that makes sense versus something that is nonsensical. The text below explores several candidates that neuroscientists are considering as this neural signature.

First, a group of neurons (a neuronal group) can fire together (or oscillate) in sync. One neuronal group may oscillate not only among its own neurons but also with the neurons in a different neuronal group. These two groups of neurons can phase-lock (oscillate together) for some time and this synchronous behavior may allow communication to take place between the two groups of neurons. Ongoing research is exploring this possibility for groups of neurons to communicate with another non-adjacent group of neurons. This type of synchronous behavior has been described as two people swinging a jump rope (Makin, 2018). They have to be in sync for the rope to rotate around smoothly.

Second, a new type of neural behavior has recently been discovered: the "traveling" wave. As cleverly described by Makin (2018), it is like doing the wave in a stadium. The wave travels. It has been found that this organized moving wave corresponds to becoming good at a cognitive task (Zhang and colleagues, 2018). In this case, they used a memory task. When people remembered something quickly, the traveling wave moves nicely across the brain, usually from the back to the front. When people were slow to recall something, the wave was either not present or less organized.

In any case, the "traveling" wave could be a strong candidate for the neural signature underlying our ordinary moments of understanding—*uni moments*. How might it work? Imagine someone's brain when they read the following introduction to my story *The Greatest Toy Ever*.

> Once upon a time, there was a HUGE toy store. It had one hundred aisles in it and each aisle was about three blocks long. The shelves went from the floor all the way to the ceiling and each shelf was filled with toys from all around the world. Now, in aisle thirty-eight…

I tell this story in front of classrooms of children and when I tell it I exaggerate my voice and gestures to match the size of the toy store. For example, the word *HUGE* is extended so it is performed as *HUUUUUUUUUUUUUUGE*. The phrase "three blocks long" is said slowly with arm gestures that show how deep these aisles might be. Similarly, the description of the shelves is matched with a squatted body position that rises up as the arms go higher when the body reaches its full height.

In this way, the large size of the toy store is supported by the long time it takes to execute certain phrases as well as the body positions and arm gestures that carve out the space. The elongated performance of certain words also hints at how long it would take you to travel down one of those aisles or climb up to reach the top shelves. As linguists say, the phrase "The shelves went from the floor" is *fictive motion*. It does not describe the shelves as a static image. Rather, it describes the movement of moving your eyes and moving your head upward to take in this incredible sight. The shelves are not moving. The observer is moving (or the observer's eyes) to take in the shelves.

Children get visibly excited when the toy store is described in this manner. The description is kind of a slow *zoom in* from the toy store as a whole to the overall number of aisles to each aisle to the shelves in each aisle. Each sentence and each phrase adds a new detail that is integrated into the image.

An intriguing hypothesis is that as each new detail is incorporated into a coherent image of the toy store, a pulsing, repeating traveling wave from, most likely, the back of the brain to the front intensifies and becomes even cleaner and more organized. This hypothesis will need much further testing. But there is a deep intuition among neuroscientists that a nonsensical or ill-fitting idea corresponds to disordered neural activity, while a sensible and coherent idea corresponds to orderly neural activity at some large level that encompasses much of the brain.

NEURAL ACTIVITY IN MAZES

The neural activity of rats learning mazes sheds some light on the orderly neural behavior during learning. The rats learning the mazes had tiny electrodes implanted to monitor their activity both during maze exploration and sleeping some time afterward. Neural activity during sleep seemed to replay the sequence of moves through the maze. The neural activity could also present variations as if the maze was being traversed backward or nearby unexplored areas were being "explored" during sleep. Overall, it is thought that this activity relates to developing a cognitive map of the maze.

The quick adjustments of the maze's map as the rat moves around it is called *remapping* and we humans engage in this process as we learn to traverse our workplace or neighborhood. We have to update our position in our internal map so we can determine how to get to where we want to go. The hippocampus is intimately involved in spatial memory, as it is in all memories. But a nearby structure called the entorhinal cortex is involved in remapping on the fly as we move around (Strange and colleagues, 2014).

The entorhinal cortex is involved with various aspects of the cognitive spatial map; but importantly here, it is involved with spatial scale—as is the hippocampus. Activity at the backend of the hippocampus is related to a very *zoomed in* detailed perspective of the map. Activity toward the front end of the hippocampus corresponds to a broad, *zoomed out* perspective of the map. A careful study shows that for rats, the activity at the *zoomed in* end of the hippocampus relates to a region of about one meter wide in the real world, while activity on the *zoomed out* end relates to a region of about ten meters wide (Strange and colleagues, 2014).

The collaboration of the entorhinal cortex and the hippocampus are associated with our abilities to zoom in, zoom out, and move around in a familiar space without getting confused. This ability can also be applied to an imagined place in your future, a remembered place from your past, or a fictional place from a novel or video game. It is not confined to the place you are currently in.

Amazingly, this *zooming* ability not only applies to spatial situations, but also to other situations where one can move from fine-grained detail to the *big picture* (Collins and colleagues, 2015). Participants watched four videos that were accompanied by various soundtracks. When the soundtrack encouraged the people to focus on the details of the video they were watching, then the backend of the hippocampus was active, which corresponds to the *zoomed in* perspective. When the soundtrack focused on linking two of the videos together, then activity progressed from the backend to the middle of the hippocampus. And when the soundtrack focused on linking all four videos, then the activity was at the *zoomed out* perspective—the front end of the hippocampus.

This phenomenon of *zooming in* and *zooming out* seems to involve the same brain structures when you are considering a spatial map as well as something non-spatial, such as watching a movie or learning math. In the non-spatial cases, you start with fine-grained detail but slowly move outward to process and understand the big picture. In other words, the term *the big picture* is not just a metaphor referring to the gist of a story, for example. The same brain structures are involved in understanding the gist of a story as they are for looking at a map from a high perspective.

PERSPECTIVE IMPLICITLY RESIDES IN LANGUAGE

Language does not describe the world independently of perspective. The perspective is built into the description in obvious and not so obvious ways. On the obvious end, a person might describe the *Leaning Tower of Pisa* from the traditional distance and position so that most of the tower is visible and is leaning to the right. Less obviously, consider the sentence *the stone wall goes from the top of the mountain to the bottom.* The fence is not moving but there is an implied movement in the description as it starts at the top of the mountain. In neither is the observer moving. The observer's gaze is moving!

There is an implied panning from the top of the mountain following its descending curvature to the bottom of the mountain. The listener/reader proceeds in one way or the other when the scene is constructed and understood. The text subtly instructs the listener how to select a perspective from which to view the scene and how this perspective might move in relation to the scene.

This implied movement from some perspective is called *fictive motion*. For example, consider the two sentences from Langacker (2008, p. 82).

The hill gently rises from the bank of the river.
The hill gently falls to the bank from the river.

These two sentences could easily describe the same scene. What differs is how the listener is instructed to recreate the scene. Does the viewpoint triggered in the listener/reader start at the river's edge and move upward? Or, does it start at the hilltop and move downward? Langacker (2008) calls this *sequential scanning*, but there is also what is called *summary scanning*, in which the described elements are gathered and properly placed as the listener encounters them in the sentence.

As well as scanning/panning, there is also *zooming in* and *zooming out*. The first sentence below starts from a bigger perspective and zooms into the location of the hat. The second sentence starts from a close-in perspective and zooms out to a bigger view.

Your hat is in the living room, in the closet, on the top shelf, behind the scrapbooks.
Your hat is behind the scrapbooks, on the top shelf, in the closet, in the living room.

Of course, there are other ways to describe space that guides the construction of a scene.

The hill was dotted with apple trees.
The police officers were posted all over the neighborhood.
The herd of sheep were spread out all over the pasture.

The verbs of these sentences subtly differ in how they may trigger the listener/reader's mind to populate the space with the apple trees, police officers, and sheep. Some people will probably construct the three scenes in the same way. For others, there might be nuanced differences.

INTERNAL SCANNING OF IMAGINED MAPS

Kosslyn and colleagues (2009) found that people used scanning when they memorized a map of a make-believe island and were asked to travel in their mind from one named location to another. Kosslyn and colleagues (2009) asked them to report when they reached a destination location after they left a starting location. Participants responded more slowly when the map distance was longer and reported more quickly when the two locations were close. The response time was basically proportional to the distance covered on the map.

Kosslyn's main point was that participants simulated movements in their internal image. They were not forced to scan because they could just jump immediately from one location to another like they were using the transporter from *Star Trek*. However, their behavior of responding to their own internal images did correspond to longer times for further distances, as if their images somehow resembled some aspects of a real map.

Pylyshyn (2006) argued that this did not prove that participants were using an internal image. According to Pylyshyn (2006), their internal maps were in a language-like representation scheme and their response times were influenced by how the task was explained to them. The participants acted as though they were scanning when they really were not doing so. It is a possible explanation, but this experiment has been repeated in multiple ways with similar results, so it is unlikely, in my opinion.

Pylyshyn (2006) and Fodor (1980) believe that humans have an internal language that is structured much like our public language. In fact, Fodor's classic book is called *The Language of Thought* because it puts forth the thesis that this internal language that we think in is structured pretty much like our public language.

Pylyshyn and Kosslyn engaged in an ongoing debate that lasted over a decade on whether there were internal images that corresponded to external images. Pylyshyn and Fodor's arguments predated many of the results from neuroscience. It would be much more difficult today to sustain an argument for a low-level computer-like language in our brains given the wealth of neuroscience results to the contrary.

The overwhelming evidence today is that the brain can simulate what it actually experiences. So, if you have witnessed a traffic accident, for example, you use the same brain areas in the same ways to remember the scene or imagine variations on the scene. Brain scans of seeing a picture and remembering the picture are almost identical. The same areas are active. Similarly, imagining variations of the traffic accident will produce a very similar brain scan when compared to the scan for witnessing the accident.

So, the point of Kosslyn's experiments in imagery was that humans simulate the map they had memorized and can move through it in a comparable way as they would a real map. Of course, our simulations are not as vivid as the actual experience. Some people, maybe even Pylyshyn and Fodor (I do not know), report that they have never experienced an inner image when they imagine something. Just because they are not aware of their visual activity does not mean that it is not happening. After a stroke or a bout of language-suppression, people discover that more images come into awareness. It all depends on how the various modalities relate to each other. Language seems to dominate awareness in many humans.

FILM DIRECTOR'S LANGUAGE

Instructions used by film directors were only developed since the late 1800s and early 1900s. However, these instructions were always implicit in how language triggered listeners (and readers) to move through space as they were constructing and simulating a scene.

The basic vocabulary of film directors and screenwriters consists of the following: zoom in (push), zoom out (pull), pan left, pan right, tilt up, tilt down, track, wide shot, full wide (the widest shot the lens allows), hold (stop movement), head shot, bust (chest to head), waist up, knee up, head to toe, follow shot (camera moves as the action moves), Rack Focus (change focus from something in the foreground to something in the background—or vice versa), slap zoom (zoom as fast as possible), dutch (angle the camera head one way or another), cut (hard transition from one scene to another), dissolve (slow transition from one scene to another). Further, there are many stylish ways to transition from one scene to the next.

My thesis is that much of a film director's language actually is an accurate description of the mental operations we can execute with our minds when simulating a scene. The directions involve selection of viewpoint, movement of the camera lens, and movement of the camera itself. The grammatical constructs of our public language and the way we choose to order our sentences implicitly contain film director instructions. In other words, the vocabulary of a film director is a rich and highly relevant way to describe the amazing mental operations we undergo when understanding language. It is a good tool for *cognitive linguists* and *cognitive psychologists* to use to obtain insights about the construction of mental simulations.

OTHER RELEVANT VOCABULARY
FOR MENTAL SIMULATION

Besides a film director's vocabulary, we also perform other operations on the scene that do not directly involve the camera. For example, we may insert an object into a scene or remove one. Also, we blend together two images or two scenes. To keep our filmmaking metaphor alive, some of the blending operations might be considered to take place post-production. That is, sophisticated computer programs manipulate the film images to create certain special effects that are not possible for the camera itself.

So, we add the following operations to our list of camera maneuvers.

Superimposition: Suppose you return home from vacation and just a few items seem to be out of place or even missing. You may superimpose (i.e., blend) your memory of how you left your home with what you are perceiving when you return. You may try to superimpose the memory and perception precisely and carefully over many features of the scene.

Selective Superimposition: "Which is bigger, your childhood bedroom or the bedroom of your first apartment?" You blend selected features of the scenes. The focus here is on the size feature.

Insertion of an Object/Agent into a Scene: "It's like our meadow only with a pond in it."

Removal an Object/Agent from a Scene: "It's like our meadow only without a big tree in the center."

Tweaking an Object: "Their porch is like our front porch only bigger, painted brown, and made out of a new fake-wood material." You start with one object and then adjust multiple features.

Time Lapse: Start with one scene, imagine the changes through time. "What will happen when the can of paint falls off the ladder?" (Fischer and colleagues, 2016).

SUMMARY

Cognitive Linguists study how the various facets of language correspond to the mental operations needed to understand language. In other words, words and grammatical constructs trigger loose sets of instructions for building up a scene or mental space that simulates the event or relationships of an abstract text. When understanding suddenly occurs then it is often accompanied by an *aha moment*. Kounios and Beeman (2015) has shed much light on the neural underpinnings of *aha moments*. When regular moments of understanding occur, what I call *uni moments,* neuroscientists have yet to fully disclose the neural signature that corresponds to these moments. But there are some promising candidates, including the traveling wave that coherently moves through the brain after successfully completing a task (Zhang and colleagues, 2018).

The perspective of the listener/reader is often implicit in the text. A film director's vocabulary (zoom, pan, track, etc.) plus other actions on a scene (insert an object, superimpose two scenes, etc.) comprise an important descriptive tool to understanding the dynamic relationship between language and cognition.

This rich set of vocabulary for mental simulations helps us describe the rich diversity of cognitive abilities. One person could be good at zooming in on visual features, but not on auditory features. Another could be adept at selectively superimposing two visual scenes on size but not on color. The number of possible combinations of types of mental operations and types of features is quite large. The overall result is a finely meshed net of diverse cognitive abilities that can be used to detect one's cognitive strengths.

REFERENCES

Collins, S. H. P., Milivojevic, B., & Doeller, C. F. (2015). Memory hierarchies map onto the hippocampal long axis in humans. *Nature Neuroscience,* advance online publication, doi:10.1038/nn.4138.

Fauconnier, G. (1997). *Mapping in thought and language.* Cambridge, UK: Cambridge University Press.

Fischer, J., Mikhael, J. G., Tenenbaum, J. B., & Kanwisher, N. (2016). The functional neuroanatomy of intuitive physical inference. *Proceedings of the National Academy of Sciences*, doi:10.1073/pnas.1610344113

Fodor, J. A. (1980). *The language of thought.* Cambridge, Massachusetts: Harvard University Press.

Huth, A. G., de Heer, W. A., Griffiths, T. L., Theunissen, F. E., & Gallant, J. L. (2016). Natural speech reveals the semantic maps that tile human cerebral cortex. *Nature, 532,* 453–458.

Kosslyn, S. M., Thompson, W. L., & Ganis, G. (2009). *The case for mental imagery.* Oxford University Press.

Kounious, J., & Beeman, M. (2015). *The Eureka factor: Aha moments, creative insight, and the brain.* New York: Random House.

Langacker, R. W. (2008). *Cognitive grammar: A basic introduction.* Oxford: Oxford University Press.

Makin, S. (June 28, 2018). "Traveling" brain waves may be critical for cognition. *Scientific American.* https://www.scientificamerican.com/article/traveling-brain-waves-may-be-critical-for-cognition/

Pylyshyn, Z. W. (2006). *Seeing and visualizing: It's not what you think.* Cambridge, Massachusetts: MIT Press.

Strange, B. A., Witter, M. P., Lein, E. S., & Moser, E. I. (2014). Functional organization of the hippocampal longitudinal axis. *Nature Reviews Neuroscience, 15,* 655–669.

Zhang, H., Watrous, A. J., Patel, A., & Jacobs, J. (2018). Theta and alpha oscillations are traveling waves in the human neocortex. *Neuron, 98(6),* 1269–1281.

Chapter 7

Student Baselines for
Mental Simulations

INTRODUCTION

How can we access what is going on in people minds when they hear a word or a scene? Brain scanning can currently tell us what areas are active when we hear a word or scene. So, we know when visual areas are active, the taste area is active, etc. But we don't know the content of the visual information, the taste information, etc. Attempts are being made, however, to infer what you are imagining from your brain activation patterns (Thirion and colleagues, 2006). Until that technology gets more sophisticated, we will just have to ask people what is going on in their minds when they hear a word or scene.

In doing so, we might discover a student who has an exceptional sensitivity to all the various hues, saturations, and brightnesses of color but maybe very little sensitivity for sound, for example. Maybe another student notices all the relationships among the characters in a scene, but not much about the physical space of the setting, for example. Once we know the modalities and features that each student is especially attuned to, then maybe we can devise ways to leverage those strengths. Further, maybe we can devise ways to help students notice what they tend to ignore. In any case, determining a baseline seems to be a solid way to notice strengths, biases, and weaknesses in the way a student constructs meaning when reading a narrative. The same basic approach can be adapted and applied to reading, science, or math; but that will be presented later.

In the coming year, I will be refining the tests for finding the baselines for each student. For example, consider the description of the toy store that was used in a previous chapter.

Once upon a time, there was a HUGE toy store. It had one hundred aisles in it and each aisle was about three blocks long. The shelves went from the floor all

the way to the ceiling and each shelf was filled with toys from all around the
world. Now, in aisle thirty-eight...

Ask students to describe around 25 features and associations of the toy
store after they read this description. Whatever the description makes them
think of, they should write down. Maybe one student only writes down
visual things (e.g., colors, shapes, objects). Maybe another student writes
down mainly tactile and kinesthetic things such as the texture of the shelves,
the feel of their muscles as they become tired while moving down the long
aisles, or the stretch of their arms as they try to reach a toy that is just out of
reach. Maybe another student writes down mainly auditory things such as the
music playing over the loudspeaker and how the music is interrupted with an
announcement about a sale, the squeak of shopping carts rolling down aisles,
or the noise of the battery-operated toys that talk or shoot.

Once you get your list of around 25 items, you can categorize them. You
could categorize them based on a common list of senses: vision, hearing, smell,
touch, taste, heat/cold, pain, balance, and body position awareness. Or, you
could use some of the categories of *Multiple Intelligences*: musical-rhythmic,
visuospatial, verbal-linguistic, logical-mathematical, bodily-kinesthetic, interpersonal, or intrapersonal (self-reflective knowledge). It is unknown yet which
category system will yield the most insightful information regarding individual
differences when students create their mental simulations of a scene.

The basic approach recommended here is to initially use a coarse category
system with just a few categories. I would probably start out with a combination of the senses and some of Gardner's *Multiple Intelligences*: vision, hearing, smell, touch, taste, spatial, verbal, bodily-kinesthetic, interpersonal, and
intrapersonal. Then, if a student showed a preference for just a few categories,
I would further examine them based on a more fine-grained category system.
For example, if a student often mentioned color for the visual items, I would
look deeper into hue (the actual color), saturation (the amount of grey mixed in
with the color), and brightness (the amount of white mixed in with the color).
If a student listed many sound items, I would look deeper into the components
of sound: pitch, loudness, and perhaps timbre—among other possibilities.

The main goal is to notice a student's natural preferences for how they put
together a scene. Of course, many different types of scenes need to be tried.
The toy store description is primarily visual, but a student may still ignore
many of the visual cues and concentrate on other aspects of the store. To
properly test a student's profile of what they mention, we will probably need
to give them several different types of descriptions (one that has primarily
auditory cues, one that has interpersonal cues among several people, etc.).
The interesting thing is how students will respond to each type of description.
Will a student go with the flow and mention only auditory features when only
auditory descriptions are included? Or, will the student mention primarily

visual features even though only auditory descriptions are included? If so, does this mean that the student just has a strong preference for visual information over auditory information? Or, do they have a real difficulty simulating auditory information in their internal reconstructions of a scene? There are many interesting questions that this type of testing can begin to answer.

At the end of this chapter is a list of 50 types of features that I use with engineers and designers when we are trying to innovate new versions or uses for an existing gadget. This master list of 50 feature types is not meant to be complete, but it helps people notice what they tend to overlook about an object. For example, for a rocking chair, everyone will mention something about motion—that the rocking chair moves back and forth. However, for a candle, no one we tested ever mentioned that candles are motionless when they burn (McCaffrey, 2011). In fact, no one we tested ever mentioned that the flame flickers and thus moves. Focusing on what people overlook leads to easy ways to create new accessories and versions of a candle.

For example, since people overlook motion about candles, we tried to make a candle that moves based on its dynamics. One way to do this is to use the fact that candles lose weight when they burn (another overlooked feature). Place a candle on one side of a justice-like scales and a counterweight on the other side. Poke holes on the platform that holds the candle so that the melted wax drains away and lessens the weight of the candle side. As the candle loses weight, its side of the scales moves upwards. For fun, we placed a snuffer above the candle. The candle eventually moves up into the snuffer and extinguishes itself. The *self-snuffing candle* was born and it actually works!

Perhaps, the list of 50 types of features can also be used to notice the many refined features that students use to create their mental simulations as they comprehend text. Of course, there are things on the list that humans tend not to notice very often, such as magnetic fields. But, perhaps, the list can also be handy for studies in animal cognition as there are a number of animals that are built to directly sense magnetic and electrical fields. Some migratory birds have a cell in their eyes that seems to detect the magnetic fields of the Earth. These cells assist with finding their way during migration routes. Further, some sharks have a series of sensors beneath their jawline that can detect electrical fields beneath them. These sensors help the sharks detect the beating hearts, which produce small electrical fields, of prey that are hiding beneath the sand on the ocean floor.

BASELINE ON COMMON OBJECTS

Another way to proceed is to give students the names of common objects (umbrella, candle, etc.) and ask them to list out all the features and associations they can think of for the objects. In my experience, people usually list somewhere between 25 and 40 items. Then, classify their responses initially based on sense modalities and human relations (e.g., vision, hearing, smell, touch, taste, spatial, verbal, bodily-kinesthetic, interpersonal, and intrapersonal). If there is a strong preference for one or more of the categories, then you can dig down deeper into those categories by examining many more subcategories. For example, if the visual is mentioned a great deal, then you can look for an emphasis on shape, color (hue, saturation, brightness), etc.

Suppose students are given the word *umbrella*. One student might list out all the situations in which they used an umbrella. They used an umbrella in London when they were trying to get back to the family's hotel. They used an umbrella to keep an angry dog away from them when they were on a walk near a friend's house. This student associates *umbrella* and possibly other common objects with episodes that involved that object. They may either not fully understand the task that they can just list features of the umbrella, such as its color, or they may be exhibiting an extraordinary memory for events in their past life that may invite further investigation into the extent of their episodic memory abilities.

Another student might focus on the features that are common to most umbrellas—the gist of the umbrella. Still, another might focus on the features of all the various umbrellas they have actually experienced. Short umbrellas and long umbrellas. Push-button umbrellas and push-open umbrellas. Pink umbrellas and yellow umbrellas. This student stays close to the details and differences as if they had typed in *umbrella* in the *Google Images* in their mind, so to speak. They do not move toward the general idea of an umbrella. This preference for details over generalities may show itself in the student's other work. They may just have a preference for details and need encouragement to move toward the general. Or, there may be a real struggle with the gist of things—the big picture—that needs to be attended to more directly.

In any case, the profile that develops from having students list features and associations of short scene descriptions and common objects can be very helpful for unearthing strong preferences for certain sense modalities, exceptional abilities in certain modes, and struggles in other modes.

FILM DIRECTOR'S LANGUAGE

Another exercise is to have students use film director's language (e.g., zoom in, pan left) as they describe how they construct a scene. A detailed list was given in the previous chapter. First, you will have to teach your students some of the basic vocabulary. Given their fascination with films, video, and television, students tend to enjoy thinking about how a director arranges camera shots and moves from one to another.

Given the description of the toy store earlier in the chapter, each student will probably have a different way of ordering and arranging camera shots. In fact, professional directors will most likely vary in how they interpret the description and present the toy store.

Further, writers and oral storytellers rely on their audience members each creating their own unique scenes in their minds. The storyteller tells one story and each reader/listener makes it come alive in their own way by populating it with details from their own life and imagination. That is why, filmgoers often say, "The book was better." One thing they might mean is that the setting they created in their own mind was more vivid and exciting than how the film director portrayed it.

After the students learn the basics of the director's language, have them describe how they image the scene unfolding in their minds. For the toy store, one student might start out with a high shot that looks down and gives a big picture of the inside of the toy store. The initial description just mentions a "huge toy store" and is agnostic as to how it could be shown. Another student might start out with an aerial shot of the outside of the toy store building before dissolving to the inside of the store. Another student might pan from left to right while in the store to give a sense of the breadth of all the aisles. Another could move (i.e., track) rapidly past all the aisles to give a sense of its size. The potential options are extensive and that was just for the first camera move.

During repeated exercises of this sort, you may find that a student might have a strong preference for certain camera positions and certain moves. Also, you may find certain aversions for other camera operations. These may just be preferences or they may reveal something about the student's underlying neural machinery. For example, for the toy store description and any other scene description, a student might struggle to ever use a high shot that looks down upon the scene and gives the "big picture." Possibly, this student has difficulty ever seeing the big picture of a scene, story, article, or argument. Their struggle might correspond to a difficulty with the front end of their hippocampus, which is used to process the "big picture" (Collins and colleagues, 2015).

In this way, we either gain evidence of a student's preferences or we gain a clue of a possible eccentricity in the neural workings of the student. In either case, we can gain some valuable information about a student's way of thinking.

FICTIVE MOTION

As previously discussed, *fictive motion* describes sentences in which motion is implied: *The road runs through the valley* and *the fence goes from the top of the river bank to the river's edge.* In contrast, some sentences do not imply motion: *The road is in the valley* and *the fence is on the river bank.*

Matlock (2004) found that participants were slower to answer questions about *fictive motion* sentences that were part of a description about a slow trip as opposed to a fast trip, a long trip as opposed to a short trip, and a trip over difficult terrain as opposed to easy terrain. There were no differences in response time when *non-fictive motion* sentences were used (e.g., *The road is in the valley*). These results, as well as many others, suggest that *fictive motion* sentences take longer to construct and process than *non-fictive motion* sentences. Many researchers believe this suggests that we are creating an internal scene that involves motion (i.e., panning) as opposed to a static image.

It is possible that we could find students who show no timing differences or brain imaging differences between *the road runs through the valley* and *the road is in the valley.* Further, we may find students who seem to have trouble understanding and inferring things from *fictive motion* sentences. These students may have difficulty in executing a pan across a scene either because of lack of practice or a neurological issue that underlies the internal act of panning.

Through further research on language comprehension and applications to learning differences, we can continue to deepen our understanding of the various strengths and weaknesses that our students possess for processing various language constructs.

COUNTERFACTUALS

Thus far, we have focused on understanding one scene. But counterfactuals open up the possibility of dealing with more than one scene (or world) at a time. Consider the following two sentences. The first sentence opens up one world and the second sentence opens up a second world that relates back to the first.

> *My friend's childhood home is a beautiful little place far out in the country. If I were him, I would never sell it.*

With the first sentence, we have a world that might contain a great number of trees. Or, the text might induce a flat expanse of farmland filled with ripening crops. It all depends on the reader's experience of the country.

Our minds could also remain at a general level of suspension by having multiple scenarios partially activated at the same time. What the mind can do resembles the field of quantum physics, in which a particle can supposedly be in multiple states at the same time until an observer comes along and forces it to choose one of the states (the Copenhagen interpretation of quantum mechanics). Our minds can do something similar as many interpretations of words and longer texts are activated until further text helps us narrow down the choices.

According to Fauconnier (1997), the second sentence of the description above then does something possibly even stranger. Triggered by the phrase "If I were you," a second world may open up in which the writer of the description and his friend are the same person. In the diagrams used by Fauconnier and other cognitive linguists, two spaces are opened up and a mapping exists between the two worlds that links the writer of the text to his friend. Now, the reader must manage which information fleshes out which world and how the items of the two worlds relate to each other.

Certainly, managing two worlds and their interrelations can get very complex and students may be fine with one world but struggle with multiple worlds. The need for a second world can be triggered by just a single word. In the following example, that word is *maybe*.

Maybe that rock in the river is a turtle.

Suddenly, there is something in the river and it could be a rock or a turtle. In one way, two worlds open up and we stay with these two co-existing worlds until further evidence helps us get back to one world. Or possibly, yet a third world opens up when we realize that the "rock" is a clamshell that was covered with moss. This way of talking also resembles quantum physics, again the Copenhagen interpretation, in which multiple worlds partially co-exist until something occurs to help us pick out which of the worlds we are in.

The main point is that linguists need to go through complex gyrations to describe how text can be understandable. They posit that multiple mental spaces—what I have been calling *worlds*—come into existence in our minds. We maintain and update these multiple mental spaces until, hopefully, we know which one we are in. A new mental space can be triggered by very short phrases such as the following: *Maybe, If I were you, She believes, He thinks.*

Some students may struggle while managing multiple mental spaces. A student may have trouble whenever the word *maybe* appears in text. This student may be able to easily read the word and recite its definition, but labor to open up a second mental space that will hold the relevant information of the second world. Or, *If I were you* may stymie a student's understanding but rephrasing it simply to *I would advise my friend* might lessen some of the confusion.

In sum, the work of Fauconnier on counterfactuals and his diagrams of multiple circles for multiple mental spaces with connecting lines between them could be very helpful to teachers and students. It could help diagnose a student's comprehension issues with counterfactuals and could supply a way to understand them better. Further, these spatial diagrams may help us understand some of the machinations the mind needs to go through in order to understand some of the constructs we come upon in our language.

Finally, the terms *mental space* and *world,* used by linguists, suggest that we humans might understand everything in terms of space—even abstract things. In our youngest years, we became thoroughly adept at navigating through physical space and all of our experience with the world takes place within space. Perhaps, our constant experience with space even grounds our understanding of more abstract things, such as math.

ABSTRACT SPACES IN MATH

The notion of numbers is taught to our students as if they reside on a number line in which the smaller numbers are toward the left and the larger numbers are toward the right. When we move to two dimensions, a second number line perpendicular to the first has the smaller numbers beneath the larger numbers. In this way, we have *spatialized* numbers.

It does not have to be this way. We could have chosen the opposite directions to present largeness and smallness. More radically, an exceptional math talent, Colleen (a pseudonym), who will be discussed in detail in a later chapter, spatializes numbers very differently. Colleen has made incredible progress on several classic unsolved math problems. Her way of spatializing numbers may help some students learn better and help professional mathematicians solve more problems.

The math world is permeated with the notion of space. There are Euclidean spaces, topological spaces, metric spaces, Hilbert spaces, to name a few. In math, the notion of space has become very general. Basically, a mathematical space consists of a group of mathematical objects that have one or more relationships among them. The mathematical objects are considered points in the space. If you can measure the distance between any two points, then it is considered a metric space. If you cannot measure distance but still have a notion of closeness between points, then you have a topological space. In sum, the notion of space, however general, still looms even within the most abstract facets of mathematics.

Even further, *Venn diagrams* have been used to spatially represent our reasoning of how groups of items relate to each other. Basically, this is applying the mathematical topic of set theory to our reasoning. One of the most famous applications is with the method of reasoning called syllogisms: *Socrates is a human; All humans are mortal; Therefore, Socrates is mortal.*

More generally, concept maps are a way to represent knowledge. A central idea is placed in a circle and associated ideas, also placed in circles, are connected to the central idea with lines. The associated ideas can also have lines connecting them to other ideas. This general spatial structure has been widely used to represent relations within human knowledge.

Building upon the seemingly inherent notion of space among so many human cognitive operations, there is an extensive literature on how teachers can leverage students' underlying notion of space to facilitate their learning (Novak, 2009).

SUMMARY

The human brain creates a simulation as it processes the text it encounters. It reuses the same brain areas as if it were perceptually experiencing the scene. The simulations are generally muted, partial, and not as vivid as perceptual experience. Understanding how a student simulates the text they encounter can shed insight into their cognitive preferences, strengths, weaknesses, as well as neural strengths and weaknesses. The use of feature lists and film directors' language can be used to this end. *Fictive motion* and counterfactuals are two examples of grammatical constructs that trigger particular neural operations during the simulation process. Understanding the neural operations involved in understanding grammatical constructs can help teachers craft ways to help students with certain comprehension issues. This mapping of grammatical constructs to neural operations has great potential for demystifying some of our students' comprehension issues.

Finally, not only does understanding narrative text depend on our ability to mentally manipulate space but understanding abstract topics such as math also relies on how well we can mentally manipulate a very general notion of space. Diagrams have been developed (e.g., Venn diagrams and concept maps) that can help students "see" even abstract knowledge and relationships in a spatial form (Table 7.1).

Table 7.1   50 Types of Features (50 Viewing Lenses)

Name	Description	Example (Based on a Plastic Chair)
Parts (Start of Static Physical Features)	Identifiable components of focal entity	Legs
Material	Material make-up of focal entity or its parts	Legs are metal
Shape	Overall shape of focal entity or its parts	Legs are U-shaped cylinders
Size (dimensional)	Length, width, depth of focal entity or its parts	Legs are about 4 feet long and have a diameter of 2 inches
Color	of focal entity or its parts	Legs are yellow
State of Matter	(Solid, liquid, gas, plasma) of focal entity or its parts	Legs are solid
Connectivity among Parts	Physical connection among components of the focal entity. This feature is based on the chair when it is *not* being used. An inert chair possesses this feature of its parts being connected in some way	The legs are connected to the seat
Spatial Relations among Parts	Distance and direction of one component to another of the focal entity. Again, this feature is based on the chair when it is *not* being used. An inert chair possesses this feature of their being spatial relations among the parts	The bottoms of all four legs form a plane
Mass	of focal entity or its parts	The mass of the chair
Weight	of focal entity or its parts	A U-shaped leg weighs about 1 pound
Number	Number of components of a certain kind of the focal entity of its parts	2 legs (because of the U-shape)
Symmetry	An important but often overlooked characteristic of the shape of a focal entity	Legs are symmetrical in two dimensions
Variety/ Homogeneity	Whether a portion of a focal entity is made of the same substance or made of a variety of substances	The legs of the chair made of plastic and are thus homogenous
Inside/Outside	The interior of a focal entity as contrasted with its exterior	The chair does not have an inside
Texture	of focal entity or its parts	Legs are smooth
Taste	how the focal entity tastes	Legs of chair do not taste good
Aroma	of focal entity or its parts	No aroma for legs

Name	Description	Example (Based on a Plastic Chair)
Thermal characteristics (Start of Dynamic Physical Features)	Temperature, conductivity, thermal capacity, radiance, etc.	Static characteristics of the plastic
Optical characteristics	absorption, reflectivity, brightness, contrast, etc.	Static characteristics of the plastic
Force characteristics	speed, momentum, tension, pressure, balance, friction, gravity, centrifugal, centripetal, torque, angular velocity, linear velocity, vibration	Static characteristics of the chair
Durability characteristics	strength, toughness	Static characteristics of the plastic
Acoustic characteristics	volume, vibration, etc.	
Chemical characteristics	Composition, reaction rate, etc.	
Electrical characteristics	current, resistance, amps, etc.	
Magnetic characteristics	strength, pole	
Radioactive characteristics	decay rate, intensity	
Fluid characteristics	buoyancy, current, pressure, flow rate, etc.	None
Side Effects (Start of Relational Physical Features)	Other effects besides the desired ones that are produced while the focal entity is in use	A side effect of sitting in a chair is the pressure of the legs on the floor. If used in the same place on the floor, over time this pressure can create indentations on the floor
Synonyms (based on use)	Other entities that can achieve the same use as the focal entity	Other objects (not subordinates) that can be sat on in a pinch. Examples: a large flat rock, a kitchen counter, a coffee table
Equipmental Partners	Environmental entities that the focal entity is used with during a particular use	A chair is often used with a table or a desk
Human Use	How a human physically manipulates the focal entity or its parts during a particular use	To sit in a chair requires a complex motor movement that involves bending the knees so that the seat of the person lands on the seat of the chair

(Continued)

Table 7.1   Continued

Name	Description	Example (Based on a Plastic Chair)
External Relations	Relations of focal entity to environmental entities during a particular use of the focal entity	The seat of the chair relates to the seat of a person when the chair is being sat upon by the person
Place/Where	The typical physical locations that the focal entity resides in during a particular use	Chairs often appear in kitchens, dining rooms, offices, on decks, etc.
Occasion/When	The typical contexts that a focal entity resides in during a particular use	Chairs are present during a family meal or a cookout on one's deck
Energy Types	During a particular use, the types of energy in play both within the focal entity as well as within and among the environmental entities: human, acoustic, biological, chemical, electrical, electromagnetic, hydraulic, magnetic, mechanical, pneumatic, radioactive, thermal	Because the chair is plastic, static electricity often builds up between the chair surface and the clothes of the person using the chair
Force Types	Gravity, centrifugal, centripetal, etc.	The chair's mass interacts with gravity to produce weight
Proximity in Space	The spatial distance and configuration of the focal entity to other environmental entities	The chair is positioned behind the desk
Orientation in Space	The spatial orientation required for the focal entity to achieve its use (a very important sub-case of overall spatial relations)	In order to be sat upon, the chair is upright; that is, the seat of the chair is above the legs
Time/Temporal Relations	The typical time-frame (milliseconds, hours) that a focal entity occupies during a particular use	An occasion of sitting can commonly last between several minutes to a couple of hours
Motion	The typical type of motion engaged in by a focal entity during a particular use	A chair is generally motionless when it is being sat upon
Permanence/Transience	How long the focal entity tends to last as it is used	A chair is usually designed to last for many years
Perspective of Human User	The typical physical viewing point that a human takes with respect to the focal entity during a particular use	A person of views the chair from a vantage point of several feet above the chair and several to many feet away from the chair. The typical perspective shapes what parts of the chair people tend to notice and which parts they overlook

Name	Description	Example (Based on a Plastic Chair)
Environmental Conditions	Humidity, Barometric Pressure, Air Conditions, Atmospheric Conditions	The chair was left in high humidity and the legs warped
Emotional Response	The emotional response that the focal entity tends to elicit. This may differ from person to person	The chair triggered sadness in her because her deceased mother always sat in that chair
Causal Relations	During a particular use, the cause-effect sequence set off among the parts of the focal entity as well as those between the focal entity and its environmental entities	When a person sits on a chair, the weight is fairly evenly distributed across the chair's seat. The weight stresses the connecting points between chair seat and the legs (etc.)
Superordinate	The more general classification of the focal entity based on its typical use	Based on its designed use, the superordinate of a chair is furniture
Subordinates	More specific version of the focal entity based on its typical use	Based on its designed use, a subordinate of a chair is a rocking chair or a bench
External Relations	Relations of focal entity to environmental entities during a particular use of the focal entity	The seat of the chair relates to the seat of a person when the chair is being sat upon by the person
Aesthetics	Artistic responses of wonder, etc.	The chair was beautiful
Thickness	of the focal entity	Chair seat is thin

REFERENCES

Collins, S. H. P., Milivojevic, B., & Doeller, C. F. (2015). Memory hierarchies map onto the hippocampal long axis in humans. *Nature Neuroscience,* advance online publication, doi:10.1038/nn.4138.

Fauconnier, G. (1997). *Mapping in thought and language.* Cambridge, UK: Cambridge University Press.

McCaffrey, A. J. (2011). The *Obscure Features Hypothesis* for innovation: One key to improving human innovation. Unpublished doctoral dissertation, University of Massachusetts Amherst.

Matlock, T. (2004). Fictive motion as cognitive simulation. *Memory and Cognition, 32(8),* 1389–1400.

Novak, J. D. (2009). *Learning, creating, and using knowledge: Concept maps as facilitative tools in schools and corporations.* London: Routledge Press.

Thirion, B., Duchesnay, E., Hubbard E., Dubois, J., Poline, J., Lebihan, D., & Dehaene, S. (2006). Inverse retinotopy: Inferring the visual content of images from brain activation patterns. *NeuroImage, 33,* 1104–1116.

Chapter 8

Gestalt Principles Revitalized

INTRODUCTION

The word g*estalt* from German translates roughly into a pattern or configuration. In the early 1900s, Gestalt Psychology was founded and focused on whole patterns in perception rather than breaking perception into its parts (Rock, 1985). Although this approach fell out of favor when Behaviorism came on the scene in psychology, still it unearthed many principles that the perceptual system seems to follow.

For example, when looking at the dot pattern on the left of Figure 8.1, people will tend to see four columns of dots. In contrast, for the right dot pattern, people see four rows of dots. This finding suggests that *proximity* makes a difference for how people group what they see. Although there are the same number of dots in each pattern, the nearness influences how we see the pattern.

Similarly, the pattern in Figure 8.2 is generally seen as five columns of dots. Although the dots are the same distance from each other both vertically and horizontally, the similarity of the open dots with each other (and the

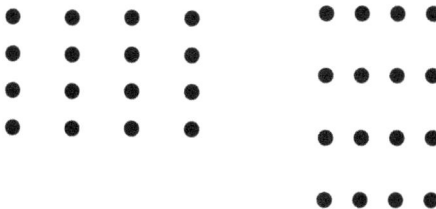

Figure 8.1   The Proximity Principle. *Source*: The author drew this figure and gives permission to Rowman & Littlefield to reprint it.

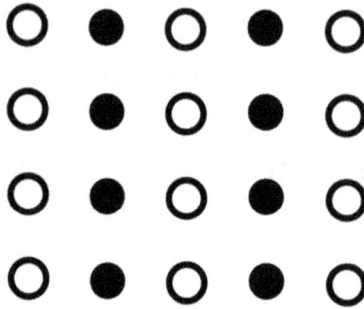

Figure 8.2 The Similarity Principle. *Source*: The author drew this figure and gives permission to Rowman & Littlefield to reprint it.

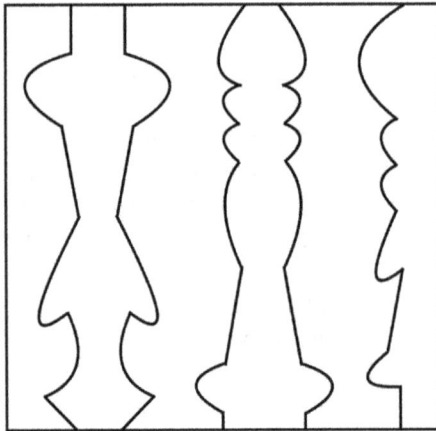

Figure 8.3 The Symmetry Principle. *Source*: The author drew this figure and gives permission to Rowman & Littlefield to reprint it.

filled-in dots with each other) will influence how we group the dots together. So, *similarity* is another principle that greatly affects how we group what we see.

Symmetry is another major principle that greatly shapes our perception. In Figure 8.3, there are five jagged lines that vertically divide the rectangle. People tend to see the space inside the symmetrical lines as an object. This symmetrical shape tends to come to the foreground while the adjacent spaces move to the background. With some effort, most people can shift their focus so that the non-symmetrical spaces seem like an object—but it usually takes a fair amount of effort. Thus, *symmetry* is another Gestalt principle that guides how we make sense of our perceptions.

Figure 8.4 contains three darkened circles with each missing a triangular slice. People tend to want *closure* and visually this shows itself as people

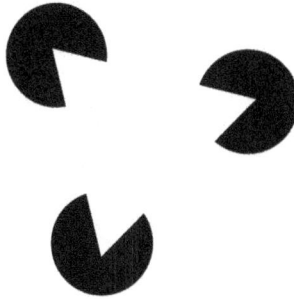

Figure 8.4 The Closure Principle. *Source*: The author drew this figure and gives permission to Rowman & Littlefield to reprint it.

Figure 8.5 Most Common Way to Count. *Source*: The author drew this figure and gives permission to Rowman & Littlefield to reprint it.

seeing a triangle between the darkened circles even though there are no lines that complete the triangle. People tend to bring a pattern to closure when possible.

What if there were people that did not follow these visual principles of grouping things together? They would certainly be unusual, but also they could be more creative because they would not have the neural habit of grouping things together in pre-determined ways. Personally, I do not presently know of people like this, but I will begin to test people in this manner. Certainly, there are people on the autism spectrum who would tend to focus on the details of the figures and not see the "gist" or pattern that most others might see.

For example, the pattern of dots in Figure 8.5 form a square. There are five columns of dots and five rows, so 5 × 5 = 25 total dots. If asked to find a path through all the dots in order to count them, most people would probably initially proceed row by row. This pathway corresponds to 5 + 5 + 5 + 5 + 5 = 25 or 5 × 5 = 25.

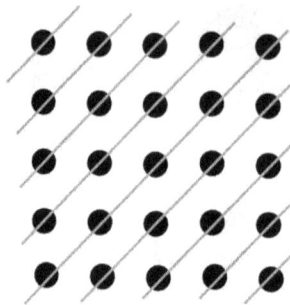

Figure 8.6   Diagonal Way to Count. *Source*: The author drew this figure and gives permission to Rowman & Littlefield to reprint it.

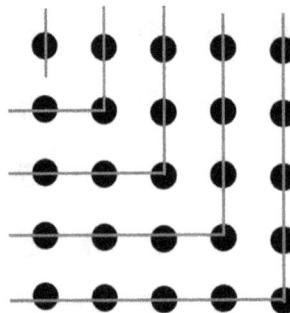

Figure 8.7   Counting in an L-Shape. *Source*: The author drew this figure and gives permission to Rowman & Littlefield to reprint it.

Based on the symmetry and simplicity of this way of looking at the dots, other interesting ways of counting up the dots might be overlooked.

Proceeding diagonally, as in Figure 8.6, yields a way to sum up a sequence of consecutive numbers that proceed upward and then come back downward: $1 + 2 + 3 + 4 + 5 + 4 + 3 + 2 + 1 = 25$. In fewer terms, $2 \times (1 + 2 + 3 + 4) + 5 = 25$.

Summing up in an L-shape, as in Figure 8.7, leads to summing up a sequence of odd numbers: $1 + 3 + 5 + 7 + 9 = 25$.

Proceeding around the outside and working your way to the center, as in Figure 8.8, yields $5 + 4 + 4 + 3 + 3 + 2 + 2 + 1 + 1 = 25$.

As in Figure 8.9, starting at the top row, then the bottom row, then the left column, then the right column, then the second row from the top, then the second row from the bottom, then the second column from the left, then the second column from the right, then finally the center yields $5 + 5 + 3 + 3 + 3 + 3 + 1 + 1 + 1 = 25$.

Finally, Figure 8.10 plays off of Figure 8.7, which adds odd numbers. Figure 8.10 adds another column, indicated by open circles, so that a new pattern emerges for adding even numbers: $2 + 4 + 6 + 8 + 10 = 30$.

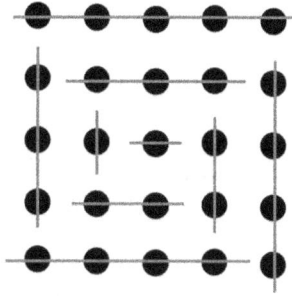

Figure 8.8 Counting from Outside In. *Source*: The author drew this figure and gives permission to Rowman & Littlefield to reprint it.

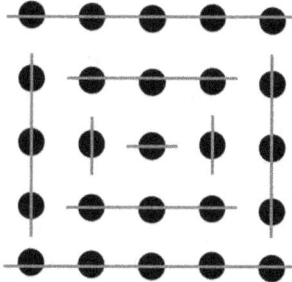

Figure 8.9 Another Way to Count. *Source*: The author drew this figure and gives permission to Rowman & Littlefield to reprint it.

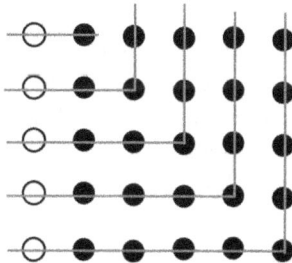

Figure 8.10 From L-Shaped Odd Counting to L-Shaped Even Counting. *Source*: The author drew this figure and gives permission to Rowman & Littlefield to reprint it.

GESTALT PRINCIPLES BLOCK OUR
ABILITY TO SOLVE PUZZLES

In the next chapter, we examine in detail an amazing math puzzle that was solved by one of my students, Dennis (a pseudonym). What makes the puzzle puzzling (or tricky) is that following the Gestalt principles of *simplicity* and *symmetry* impedes progress to a solution. For the math puzzle that Dennis solved, he had to work against simple maneuvers and make a complicated counterintuitive maneuver. Similarly, Dennis had to ignore the obvious symmetry of the problem and find a more obscure symmetry. Maybe there was no struggle for Dennis. Maybe he is not bound by these Gestalt Principles. I do not know without further testing.

In any case, puzzles are often puzzling because their solutions require working against the Gestalt Principles which influence many people.

OTHER PRINCIPLES

Continuity means that our eyes tend to track lines and curves as they move among the elements of a collection. So, in Figure 8.11, our eyes will tend to proceed from the top left dot and traverse the rest of the dot as if they were a bow that circled back on itself and ended with the top right dot. *Connectivity* means that people tend to group stimuli together that are connected—or appear connected—rather than stimuli that are disconnected.

In all cases, according to Gestalt Principles, our visual system will strongly prefer *order* and *simplicity* when it groups elements together as it tries to make sense of a scene. *Simplicity* is a vague concept and can be influenced by many factors such as symmetry, continuity, etc.

SUDOKU

The famous puzzle *Sudoku,* like many other puzzles and games, plays off of several Gestalt principles to make the game challenging. If it followed all of the principles, the puzzle would be too easy. If it pushed against all the principles, it would probably be way too difficult. If it follows some principles and goes against a few others, then the challenge should be "just right."

Figure 8.11 The Continuity Principle. *Source:* The author drew this figure and gives permission to Rowman & Littlefield to reprint it.

Sudoku challenges players to spread out the numbers 1-9 according to various rules. First, in each 3-by-3 square, each number can occur only once. Similarly, in each row across the whole board and down each full column, each number must also occur only once. This challenge of spreading out the numbers in particular ways works against the Gestalt principle of *proximity* and *similarity,* in which people would prefer all the similar numbers to be close to each other: all the 1's to be in one 3-by-3 square *(proximity),* the 2's in another square, etc. But following *similarity* and *proximity* would trivialize the puzzle and make it far too easy.

The next section shows how the puzzle, *Star Travel,* balances its use of several Gestalt principles.

Figure 8.12 is a *Star Travel* map in which each shape represents a star. You can travel from one star to another in two ways. If two stars are connected by a line, then you can travel between them. You will use your own rocket fuel so it will be costly. If two stars are the same shape, then they are connected by a wormhole and you can jump between the stars. You will not use any of your rocket fuel in this case because the wormhole does all the work.

What is the path that uses the least number of slides to travel from *Star #1* to *Star #21*? In other words, you want to jump as much as you can and slide as little as you can. There are multiple solution paths that all involve just two slides: (1) #1 jump to #25, then slide to #27, jump to #13, slide to #18, jump

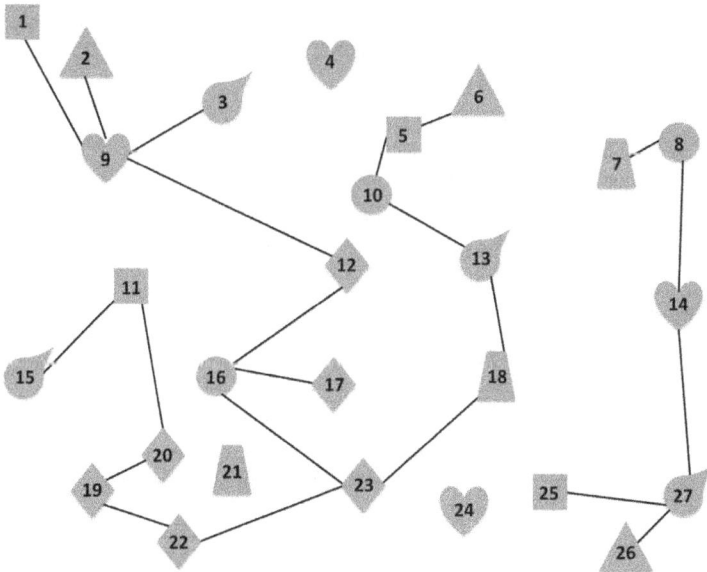

Figure 8.12   Star Travel. *Source:* The author drew this figure and gives permission to Rowman & Littlefield to reprint it.

to #21; (2) #1 slide to #11, slide to #15, jump to #13, slide to #18, jump to #21; (3) #1 jump to #5, slide to #10, jump to #8, slide to #7, jump to #21.

Students find puzzles like this engaging. This type of puzzle uses *connectivity* as one way to travel. The eye can easily follow connected lines and group them together into a path. The jumps from star to star work against the principle of *connectivity* and jumps must take place between stars of *similar* shape. Based on feedback from students, this puzzle seems to have the right balance between cooperating with Gestalt principles and working against them to make it interesting and sufficiently challenging.

GESTALT PRINCIPLES IN MATH
AND THEORETICAL PHYSICS

Mathematicians and theoretical physicists, who also use a great deal of math, often talk about the beauty of their work. Paul Dirac's words exemplify a typical quote from a physicist: "It is more important to have beauty in one's equations than to have them fit experiment" (Dirac, 1963). G. H. Hardy's quote is common for a mathematician: "The mathematician's patterns, like the painter's or the poet's must be beautiful; the ideas, like the colors or the words must fit together in a harmonious way. Beauty is the first test: there is no permanent place in this world for ugly mathematics" (Hardy, 1940).

But according to several recent writers on physics, the use of beauty as a criterion for a physics theory is misguiding physicists in their work. The criterion of *symmetry* has played a big role for a long time. Many physicists propose what is called *supersymmetry*. Each type of particle that we know of supposedly has a symmetrical type of partner that is like the original particle in certain ways and different in others (Hossenfelder, 2018). There were high expectations in 2012 at the Large Hadron Collider (LHC) in Geneva, Switzerland, when evidence for the mysterious Higgs boson finally revealed itself. Many physicists thought that the LHC would also give us evidence of some of the symmetrical particles. But it did not.

According to some physicists, the theory of *supersymmetry* is so beautiful and elegant, that it must be true—or close to it. However, Sabine Hossenfelder, a theoretical physicist, has written a book in 2018 whose title says it all for her view and the view of a growing number of other physicists: *Lost in Math: How Beauty Leads Physics Astray*. Besides covering a great deal of physics, her book also discusses cognitive biases that influence what physicists are drawn toward and what they will generally accept as an interesting theory.

Among the dozen cognitive biases she discusses, Hossenfelder reiterates our strong preference for criteria such as symmetry, simplicity, and order. These more aesthetic criteria are usually referred to generally as beauty or elegance. When there is insufficient data from the LHC to constrain our theories, the notions of beauty and elegance run rampant in guiding what a theory should look like and how it should be developed.

But what if the laws of nature are ugly? This question is dealt with in a *New Scientist* magazine article by Daniel Cossins (2018). In fact, the magazine cover with Cossins' article proclaims *Welcome to the Uglyverse: There's Nothing Beautiful about the Laws of Nature*. How would physicists and mathematicians deal with this if they one day have to face this fact? The notion of beauty is so attractive and purpose-giving for many of them that it may cause a career crisis or even a life crisis in some of them.

In any case, the Gestalt principles are alive and strong. They exert their considerable influence both at the unconscious low level of perceptual grouping and at the conscious level of deciding what math topics and physics theories to pursue.

SUMMARY

Gestalt principles of perception are not in vogue these days in the study of cognitive psychology. These principles, however, still describe very well how most people perceptually group things. The principles can greatly hinder our ability to see new patterns that may help us solve tough problems. In this way, counteracting the principles can be a source of creativity.

Many puzzles and games strike a balance between following some of these principles and fighting against other of these principles. If a puzzle or game followed all of the principles, it would probably be too trivial and thus not very interesting. Puzzles and games have to strike a balance of being orderly and simple in one way and chaotic and complex in other ways. The balance between order and chaos seems to generally make something quite interesting.

Even for professional physicists and mathematicians, these principles are highly active and fall under the terms of beauty and elegance. A growing number of thinkers believe these principles have too much sway and that math and physics will need to become more "ugly" to accurately describe our universe.

In the upcoming chapters we will look at puzzles, their simplicity and complexity, and the amazing youth who can easily solve them. Analyzing puzzles, games, and school topics can shed light on some of what makes them tricky and what hints and techniques we can use to make them more understandable.

REFERENCES

Cossins, D. (March 3–9, 2018). The ugly truth. *New Scientist, 237(3167)*, 30–33.

Dirac, P. (May 1963). The evolution of the physicist's picture of nature, *Scientific American, 208*(5), 45–53.

Hardy, G. H. (1940). *A mathematician's apology.* Cambridge: Cambridge University Press.

Hossenfelder, S. (2018). *Lost in math: How beauty leads physics astray.* New York: Basic Books.

Rock, I. (1985). *The logic of perception.* Cambridge, MA: MIT Press.

Chapter 9

From Non-linguistic to Linguistic Puzzles

INTRODUCTION

Given that we humans all start as non-linguistic beings, testing for cognitive abilities should start with non-linguistic puzzles. This beginning point will test the underlying abilities that might be present beneath our late-arriving language abilities that may be masking some amazing non-linguistic abilities.

Below, we will examine a progression of puzzles that start with those that require no accompanying verbal instructions and proceed to those that require a great deal. Animal cognition researchers need to use the non-verbal puzzles, except for the rare animal that has been intensively trained to understand some symbolic communication (e.g., Koko the gorilla and Alex the parrot).

Regarding language in puzzles, there is a difference in the type of linguistic instructions required. Stating the goal, as in "disentangle the metal pieces," is very different than stating constraints such as "you are not allowed to tip the entire box." A free-standing box can be tipped physically and an animal will not comply with this arbitrary constraint.

These different uses of language have different effects on the cognitive processes in humans. Most of the students I have worked with who have exceptional spatial abilities show a strong preference for puzzles that do not require stating such constraints. They strongly prefer puzzles that have very few or no constraints that need to be verbally described. Stating the goal briefly, such as "disentangle the metal pieces," however does not seem to bother them.

When testing animal cognition, all aspects of the problem must be completely grounded in the physical cause-effect structure of the testing device. You cannot give animals verbal instructions such as "Please don't tip the box when you are trying to get the food on the inside of it." The box must be secured so that the animal cannot tip it.

For example, in the documentary, "Beak and Brain," a raven tried to get food out of a plexiglass box. To do so, it had to drop three stones through an opening at the top of a box (Sigl and colleagues, 2013). Three stones had sufficient weight to tip a platform in the middle of the box so the food would slide down the tipped platform (along with the stones) and out of an opening at the lower side of the box. After placing the first stone in the top opening, the raven got frustrated and just tipped the entire box until the food slid out of the opening.

The experimenter then nailed the box to the wooden bench so the raven could not "cheat." In other words, the experimenter eliminated this particular cause of getting the food out. Obviously, the experimenter could not just say, "Do not tip the box." All the constraints of the puzzle had to be embodied in the way the physical puzzle worked.

Most animal cognition tests have to do with receiving food as a reward for solving a puzzle. Solving the puzzle often causes the food to become accessible to the animal. In some cases, the experimenter offers the food when the puzzle is solved, so the food reward becomes strongly associated with solving the puzzle task.

Humans can certainly understand the goal of the wordless puzzles that are given to animals. The next level for humans would be puzzles that require minimal language to explain the goal. For example, the company *Hanayama* has an extensive collection of metal puzzles that they categorize from level 1 (easy) to 6 (extremely challenging). Multiple metal parts are entangled in an intricate manner. With humans, you just hand them a puzzle and say, "Disentangle it." The goal is expressed in a minimal way. Primates could most likely be trained to work on these metal puzzles for the promise of a food reward. Many would have the necessary manual dexterity. Corvids (ravens, crows, etc.) with their claws may not have the necessary dexterity.

JOHN AND THE 3D ENTANGLED METAL PUZZLES

A student of mine, John (a pseudonym), has an uncanny ability to disentangle any metal entangled puzzle given to him. He has solved in a matter of minutes every puzzle given him from *Hanayama*, including many from level 6—the most challenging level. John has yet to find a metal puzzle that he could not solve. Several puzzles from *Hanayama* are shown in Figure 9.1.

I have asked John to explain how he solves these puzzles. He has described his thought processes to me while he has solved several of these puzzles. Honestly, I could not follow him. All of his individual words and phrases

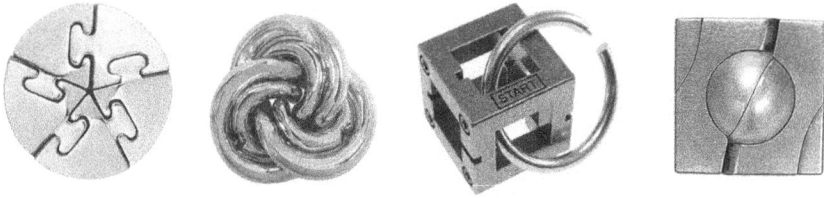

Figure 9.1 Sample Hanayama Metal Puzzles. *Source*: These metal puzzles are sold online by Hanayama Puzzles at http://www.hanayama-puzzles.co.uk/acatalog/All-puzzles.html.

made sense, but I could not understand how he decided what to try and what to focus on to free the pieces from each other. He could decipher how these three-dimensional pieces of metal weave in and out of each other and image how they could move relative to each other.

It was both exasperating and exhilarating to listen to John. Exasperating, in the sense that, like all adult humans, I have a great deal of experience navigating through three-dimensional spaces and using three-dimensional objects. Yet, I was unable to understand the descriptions of the young man before me as he narrated his manipulations of the three-dimensional objects. Exhilarating, in the sense that I was in the presence of an exceptional talent who was just doing what was so natural for him. His parents had noticed his "freakish ability," as his father described it, for all things mechanical since John was young.

John's official diagnoses are ADHD and several others struggles related to reading, learning through language, and executive functioning. Within John's standard cognitive tests in his files, especially his perceptual reasoning scores, there is nothing to indicate that he would possess such extraordinary abilities that combined his tactile, visual, and motor skills working on 3D objects.

During the time that I worked with John, he showed an exclusive preference for 3D puzzles that he could manipulate with his hands. There were many 2D puzzles available and many other spatial puzzles described on paper that required performing the manipulations exclusively in the mind. John seemed to avoid the other types of spatial puzzles as he focused on the 3D entangled puzzles. I will have to test out John's range of abilities further at a future time.

TYPES OF ATTENTION: TYPES OF ADHD

One interesting thing is that John has been diagnosed with ADHD. However, he exhibited intense attention and focus when he worked on the metal puzzles. Perhaps, John's struggles with inattentiveness, hyperactivity, and impulsivity were dependent on the type of stimuli and tasks that were involved.

Markova and McArthur have articulated such a theory. They articulate three basic types of attention: focused, sorting, and open (Markova and McArthur, 2015). Focused attention is what we normally think of as attention: maintaining concentration on the stimuli or task in front of you. Sorting attention refers to a process of moving back and forth, comparing and contrasting various things. Open attention describes a state of diffuse awareness where memories, images, and ideas transform—possibly into something new.

According to Markova and McArthur (2015), for each of us, different modalities of stimuli lead to different types of attention. Auditory, visual, and kinesthetic stimuli trigger different attentional responses. In my experience of working with John, for example, it seems that kinesthetic input triggers focused attention while auditory triggers open attention. In Markova and McArthur's theory, visual stimuli should trigger sorting attention for John, but more testing on John would be needed to confirm this.

In their system, each form of stimuli has a receptive mode and an active mode. For auditory stimuli, listening and hearing are considered receptive; while storytelling, lecturing, singing, speaking, and joke telling are active. For kinesthetic stimuli, smelling, tasting, feeling, bodily sensing of your position in space, and proprioceptive sensing of the relative position of your arms and legs are all receptive. Sports, hands-on activities, building, dancing, and moving are active. For visual stimuli, watching, reading, and seeing are receptive; while writing, editing, drawing, painting, and photographing are active.

Markova and McArthur have elaborate descriptions of what a person might be like if the kinesthetic (K) triggers focus for them, the auditory (A) triggers open attention, and the visual (V) triggers sorting attention. Further, they have detailed descriptions for the other five types: KVA, AKV, AVK, VKA, VAK. Finally, they have checklists so people can assess which of the six types they are. It is an impressive system and sheds more refined light on the diversity of human attention capabilities.

It is possible, however, that their system will need even more refinement. Perhaps, there are people who focus only when they experience taste, or smell, or emotions, or proprioceptive body positions. Further, perhaps visual stimuli should be further broken down into color, brightness, and saturation, shape, shading, etc. In any case, Markova and McArthur's system is a significant step forward in trying to understand how, when, and why humans attend.

STEVEN AND EXCEPTIONAL SPATIAL TALENT

The puzzle *Scramble Squares* just has nine pieces. As Figure 9.2 shows, each piece is square and fits together with the other square pieces in a three-by-three pattern to form a large square. The big square forms an interesting picture. In Figure 9.2, each edge of a piece contains half of a lizard—either the tail half or the head half. The goal is to get each of the lizard halves that are touching each other to form a complete, matching lizard. For example, the orange lizard tail should match up with the orange lizard head to form a whole orange lizard.

Although it required a lot of text above to fully describe a *Scramble Squares* puzzle, it is fairly simple to describe to students. Have the puzzle pieces already arranged as a large square (3 by 3 square) and just say, "Arrange the pieces to make a coherent picture. Keep the shape as a large square." The first sentence states the goal and is easy to understand when the student sees the pieces arranged as a full square. The second sentence states

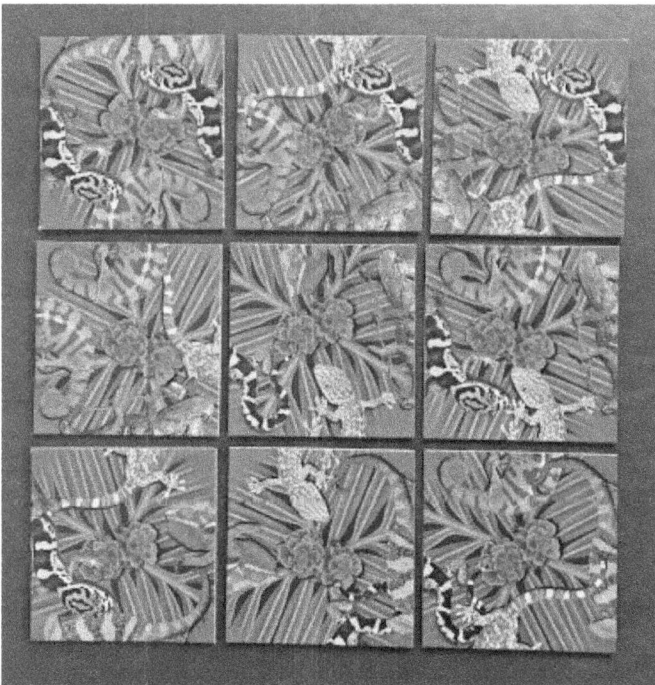

Figure 9.2 Scrambles Squares with Lizards. *Source*: Scramble Squares are produced by b.dazzle Inc. at http://www.b-dazzle.com/scramble.asp.

a constraint. This is also easy for students to understand and maintain given that they see the overall shape of the initial set-up of the pieces.

The number of possible arrangements of these nine pieces is astronomically large: just over 95 billion. Each piece can be in 9 different locations: 3 rows times 3 columns, or 9 possible locations. All 9 pieces can be placed in 9! (or $9 \times 8 \times 7 \times 6 \times 5 \times 4 \times 3 \times 2 \times 1 = 362,880$) possible arrangements. However, once a piece is in a position, it can be rotated in place to achieve 4 different orientations. Rotating each of the 9 pieces results in 4 to the 9th power or 262,144 possibilities for each placement of the 9 pieces. So, $362,880 \times 262,144 = 95,126,814,720$ (or just over 95 billion) total possible arrangements.

Scramble Squares is incredibly difficult to solve. There is only ONE CORRECT arrangement and over 95 billion incorrect arrangements. However, a person solving this puzzle would not intentionally place a piece in which the lizard halves did not match up. Taking this into account reduces the number of possible arrangements to just over 40 billion. Still, this puzzle is incredibly difficult to solve.

Steven (a pseudonym) solved this lizard version of the *Scramble Squares* puzzle in about five minutes the first time he tried it. Amazing! Steven did not know he had this ability and he was very dismissive. He basically said, "I got lucky!" I assured him he did not, but he continued to downplay his accomplishment. So, I took the 9 lizard squares, thoroughly mixed them up behind my back, and gave him the mixed-up puzzle again. Steven solved it again this time in about 10 minutes. Still, Steven continued to disregard his accomplishment.

This kind of spatial ability is never needed in normal schooling. So, it is not surprising that Steven did not know he had this ability. Neither would such a demanding test of spatial ability be involved in most neuropsychological assessments, so if Steven had taken such an assessment he most likely would not have a clue that he possessed such an ability.

It is discouraging that Steven would so easily downplay and disregard his ability. Since it was never rewarded in school, this means that the normal curriculum does not value such an ability. Since normal schools do not value it, then it makes sense that Steven had learned what schools valued and spatial ability was not in that list of valuable skills. In fact, even after such an extraordinary ability is discovered, schools would still have to create moments in school where this skill would be used and valued. They do not readily exist.

In fact, the only "school lesson" I could initially think of was to teach Steven the basics of the online protein folding game called *FoldIt*. The plan is to have this happen next school year when I continue to work with Steven.

FoldIt originated from the following scenario. Scientists had been stumped for over a decade regarding the 3D structure of a protein-cutting enzyme related to an AIDS-like virus (University of Washington, 2011). This class of enzymes plays a critical role in how the AIDS virus propagates. Understanding this aspect of the AIDS virus was crucial to knowing how to control and combat it.

Once this problem was implemented in the online game *FoldIt*, gamers took over where scientists had failed. It took the gamers only three weeks to solve it. That is, the gamers devised a sufficiently accurate 3D model that the scientists could then refine and from there they could begin to design retroviral drugs, including AIDS drugs.

The *FoldIt* game allows people without biochemical expertise but with exceptional 3D pattern matching skills to contribute to this important research. According to the researchers at the University of Washington, where the *FoldIt* game was created, this was the first time that gamers solved an unsolved scientific problem (University of Washington, 2011). Based on this success, *FoldIt* is still an active platform and gamers can use their 3D spatial skills to help solve problems relevant to cancer, Alzheimer's disease, immune deficiencies, among other medical research.

It is quite plausible that people untrained in biochemistry may have significantly better spatial abilities than expert biochemists. Biochemists definitely need a certain degree of spatial ability to make it through their training, which deals with 3D molecules, proteins, enzymes, etc. However, there is no assurance that the best spatial reasoners are in the biochemistry field. Extraordinary spatial reasoners could reside in many different fields: architecture, geology, archaeology, mathematics, astrophysics, to name a few. Or, exceptional spatial reasoning could reside in high school students (or younger) who have yet to decide their field of study. Or, brilliant spatial skills could reside in high school students (or younger) who struggle with some of the basic skills that their schooling requires; but they could still help make important scientific contributions if given the chance.

I imagine a career that does not exist yet called a *Spatialist* that helps solve tough spatial problems no matter where they come from. One day, our young *Spatialist* may help a shipping company minimize the wasted space in their shipping boxes. The next day, they are helping a geologist imagine how the layers of sediment over eons reconfigured itself after several large, historic earthquakes. The next, they are helping imagine a new way that the Egyptian pyramids were built based upon the structure of their inner passageways. The next, they are helping an astrophysicist imagine a new way that space-time could fold to create a portal from one region of space to another. The next, they are helping the company *Hanayama* design a new line of entangled metal puzzles.

In none of these cases does our *Spatialist* need to be a content expert in shipping, geology, Egyptology, astrophysics, or puzzle-making. They just need to use their extraordinary gift. But in order to do that, they first need to discover it. They need to have it tested for in schools. They need to have the characteristics of their skill understood. Is their gift focused on 3D objects and images? Or, does it extend to higher dimensions such as projections of 4D objects into 3D space? Perhaps, their spatial ability shines in the masterful manipulation of 2D images and does not extend up to 3D. Do they need to manipulate the objects with their hands like John seems to? Or, can they do it in their minds?

When asked, Steven was unable to articulate what he does to solve the *Scramble Squares* puzzles. He does not seem to have access to his inner spatial workings. Like Lisa, another exceptional spatial talent described later, he just seems to "see" the answer. He just seems to "see" when he is close to arranging the pieces correctly. John, on the other hand, could articulate something of what he considered and how he proceeded with the 3D metal puzzles. John's description, however, may not be very accurate as often happens when we give reasons in hindsight for our behavior to make it appear reasonable to ourselves and others (Kahneman, 2013). Our description of how we completed an action may be different from what our brain actually did. We are not lying. We just do not have accurate access to this level of neural processing.

For example, a classic experiment by McCloskey (1983) demonstrated that people have great difficulty determining the path to the ground of a ball when it is dropped from a plane flying at a constant speed. Given a diagram of a plane moving from left to right, people were to draw a line showing the path the ball will take as it travels to the ground. Correct answers were given by only 40 percent of the people. The line on the right shows the correct shape of the ball's path to the ground (Figure 9.3).

However, nearly all the students in my classrooms over the years could successfully perform the following related task. Given a ball, they would run

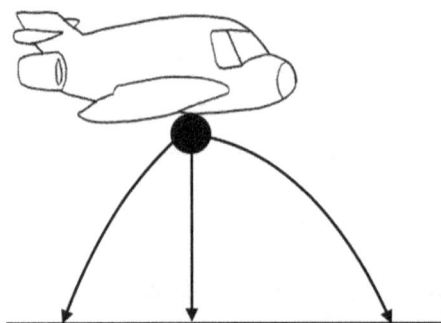

Figure 9.3   Plane Dropping Ball. *Source*: The author drew this figure and gives permission to Rowman & Littlefield to reprint it.

quickly across the classroom and run by a trashcan. They would try to release the ball so it would land in the trashcan. We even had students pushing other students at high speeds past the trashcan on the teacher's chair, which has wheels. Their visual-motor systems knew when to release the ball so that it would arc down into the trashcan.

Why do so many fail the test on paper but can act it out accurately and almost effortlessly? Several things might be going on. The coordination between our vision and motor systems is intricate and, quite often, very accurate. These systems "knew" that the ball had to be released before you reached the trashcan. An analysis of the situation based on the pictures does not generally contain this information. Even if the people do a simulation in their minds of the fast flying plane, still their inner simulations most often do not have this information.

Further, in the diagrams we are looking at the plane from the outside and watching it act from a distance. When we perform the action, we are acting it out from the inside, so to speak. This is not a trivial difference. Our visual and motor systems use different coordinate systems depending on the situation. Egocentric coordinates have us positioned in the center of the action. We would use this scheme when we are running toward the trashcan. Allocentric (i.e., exocentric) coordinates, on the other hand, are used for objects outside of us and how they move and act independent of us. We would use this scheme for thinking about the plane and the ball. The information in one mode of presenting the situation is not necessarily present in the other mode.

Regarding the spatial puzzles, a person who is very clumsy still could be fantastic at solving certain spatial puzzles. One reason among others would be that a puzzle like *Scramble Squares* triggers the use of allocentric coordinates, while moving through the world and picking up things mostly relies on egocentric coordinates. Further, a person who easily gets lost when given directions might still be exceptional at certain spatial puzzles. There is no disconnect. The two use different coordinate systems.

Finally, professional baseball players and tennis players may be able to say very little about how they can accurately hit a ball traveling and curving at such high speeds. Our language abilities probably have very little access to the visual and spatial information at this level of neural processing. The same applies to John and Steven's inability to describe what they are doing. In John's case, he may have been under the illusion that he was giving an accurate description. This requires further testing, which I plan to carry out in the future.

As a species, the workings of our visual system long predated any linguistic ability. Similarly, our individual visual system was operating in sophisticated ways before we acquired language to describe what we visually experience. It makes sense that some or most of our inner neural processing is only partially or almost totally inaccessible to our descriptions. Even more, our descriptions may be highly inaccurate compared to what is actually going on. Why should a baseball player be able to reach down and accurately describe when they decide to swing the bat at a pitch? In fact, language itself may be actually distancing us from being aware of the experiences happening to us through our sense modalities. As a stroke victim, Jill Bolte Taylor, became aware of so much more when her language ability was silenced. I became aware of so much more when I habitually engaged in a language-suppression technique for a week.

COMPANIES ARE AHEAD OF SCHOOLS

The desire to hire people who think differently is growing. The *Harvard Business Review* published a 2017 article, *Neurodiversity as a Competitive Advantage* (Austin and Pisano, 2017), which discussed how a growing number of companies are now changing their hiring practices. These businesses were finding that people with learning differences had some incredible skills that the companies badly needed. But these same people were having trouble making it through the interview process. As part of their changes, these companies were also providing assistance to these new hires to help them with some of their weaker skills.

Given this context, it is exciting to share that my EHS students easily out-innovated a roomful of 20 high-tech PhD researchers when I gave both an *aha problem*. With an *aha problem*, people generally get stuck until they notice an obscure feature that then illuminates a solution.

However, a significant number of EHS students consistently solve these puzzles without getting stuck. That is, they do not initially give a wrong answer, have to be told why that answer will not work, become stymied for a good while, and then suddenly notice the overlooked feature that leads to the correct solution. Rather, they often come directly to the correct solution as their first answer with little or no hesitation. For the *aha problem* given to both the adult researchers and EHS students, 26 percent of the EHS students solved it in this direct manner without getting stuck while 43 percent solved it overall. In contrast, only one researcher solved the problem at all—just a 5 percent solution rate. For comparison, only two of the 98 public school teens tested solved the problem directly without first giving a wrong answer (a 2 percent solution rate) and 28 percent solved it overall.

Why are there such differences in performance? For high-tech researchers, they tend to be exceptional analytic thinkers. But innovation requires thinking differently to notice what has been overlooked and then using it creatively to solve the problem.

Comparing youth to adults, it is believed that somewhere within the age range of pre-teen to teen, youth are in a cognitive "sweet spot," in which they can still make the wild associations of a child but are beginning to be able to assess their idea's plausibility like an adult.

But beyond this general advantage of youth, our EHS youth do have a definite but often hidden advantage. By the time our students finally find EHS, their files are filled with the results of many educational and psychological tests. These tests primarily inform them of their deficits as well as any "normal" skills they possess. Blatantly absent from their files are most of their "exceptional" abilities that can be leveraged toward academic achievement and ultimately real-world success.

Schools need to catch up to companies. Companies may not have all the tools they need to recognize people with exceptional talents. But, at least, companies are beginning to recognize the need to find these people so the company has the thinking skills it needs to succeed.

But schools need to catch up. First, schools need to be aware of the changing trend of the skills that companies are looking for. Second, schools need to develop ways to detect these desirable skills and then develop them even further.

It is my hope that this book helps provide some of the tools needed to first detect and then develop the exceptional talents of our learning diverse youth.

SUMMARY

This chapter began with a description of a progression of puzzles from non-linguistic puzzles to minimally linguistic ones. As a species, our late-arriving linguistic abilities may be hiding some of our greatest skills. Our own brains may have amazing abilities that the onset of language as a child partially masked over. Two case studies were presented of the exceptional talents of my students John and Steven. Companies are beginning to recognize their needs for these diverse abilities. Our schools need to do a better job of recognizing and then developing these skills. The next chapter will continue our progression to puzzles requiring more verbal description, as well as presenting further case studies.

REFERENCES

Austin, R. D., & Pisano, G. P. (May–June, 2017). Neurodiversity as a competitive advantage. *Harvard Business Review,* 96–103. https://hbr.org/2017/05/neurodiversity-as-a-competitive-advantage

Kahneman, D. (2013). *Thinking, Fast and Slow*. New York: Farrar, Straus and Giroux.

Markova, D., & McArthur, A. (2015). *Collaborative intelligence: Thinking with people who think differently*. New York: Spiegel and Grau.

McCloskey, M. (1983). Naive theories of motion. In D. Gentner & A. L. Stevens (Eds.), *Mental models* (pp. 299–324). Hillsdale, NJ: Erlbaum.

Sigl, A. (Producer), Arzt, V., & Sigl, A. (Directors). (2013). *Beak and Brain: Genius Birds from Down Under*. Germany: Text Und Bild.

University of Washington. (2011, September 19). Gamers succeed where scientists fail: Molecular structure of retrovirus enzyme solved, doors open to new AIDS drug design. *ScienceDaily*. Retrieved July 15, 2018, from www.sciencedaily.com/releases/2011/09/110918144955.htm

Chapter 10

More Impressive Spatialists

INTRODUCTION

In this chapter, we look at another student with exceptional spatial ability and an adult who has both impressive spatial and mathematical ability. One difference between the two is that the adult, who has been aware of her gifts for a longer period of time, can reflect better upon their inner workings and how to best relate to them.

LISA THE SPATIALIST

Lisa (a pseudonym), who was briefly mentioned in the previous chapter, solved several versions of the *Scramble Squares* puzzle. She solved the version with the lizard images, the candy images, and the planet images. She solved each one in somewhere between five to ten minutes. She never failed.

When asked how she proceeded when working on these problems, she basically had nothing to say. She said it was easy for her. Her parents had noticed some of her special abilities before; but, once again, there was really no place for these abilities to shine in a normal school setting.

Lisa solved at least four different types of very difficult spatial puzzles. Only one other type will be described here.

Figure 10.1 shows the *Gordian Knot* in its tangled and disentangled forms, which is comprised of six pieces. According to the booklet that accompanies this puzzle, separating the pieces requires the execution of 69 maneuvers in the correct order. One day in class, Lisa was handed the fully entangled *Gordian Knot* on the left of Figure 10.1 and invited to "Disentangle it." She took just twenty minutes to separate all of the pieces to produce the right of

Figure 10.1 Gordian Knot Entangled and Untangled. *Source*: The Gordian Knot is produced by ThinkFun at https://www.thinkfun.com/products/gordians-knot/.

Figure 10.1. The booklet was well hidden away from her. The next day in class, she reassembled all of the pieces into their original entangled form. It was amazing to witness this!

I know what you are thinking. Did John ever try the *Gordian Knot*? Not yet. I bought this puzzle after my class with John had ended, but I plan to have him try it in the future.

Lisa always exhibited a strong preference for spatial puzzles that required little or no accompanying description. Like John in the previous chapter, she showed no interest in the many spatial puzzles on paper that came with a diagram and sometimes a fair amount of text that articulated the moves that were permitted and the moves that were not. My hypothesis is that Lisa excelled with physical puzzles that could be manipulated instead of just thinking about a static diagram on paper. Also, she only showed interest if the accompanying description was brief, such as "Disentangle this" for entangled puzzles or "Make a nice picture" for the *Scramble Squares*.

It may be possible that she would have trouble doing the manipulations in her mind or holding many constraints in her mind (e.g., "You cannot make the following moves"). I do not know and would have to test it out. I just know that I was often surprised by which puzzles she would dive into and which she would reject. Then, I began to notice a pattern.

In contrast to the teens who had trouble articulating their inner life, I had the privilege of encountering an adult with extraordinary spatial and mathematical abilities. Her name is Colleen (a pseudonym). She approached the administration of our school, where one of her children attended, and asked them if they would connect her with someone in the math department who had experience with publishing proofs. She had some math proofs that she would like to show someone. Since I had published a math proof earlier that year, they approached me and I was happy to talk with her. She ended up presenting me with proofs to several classic unsolved math problems.

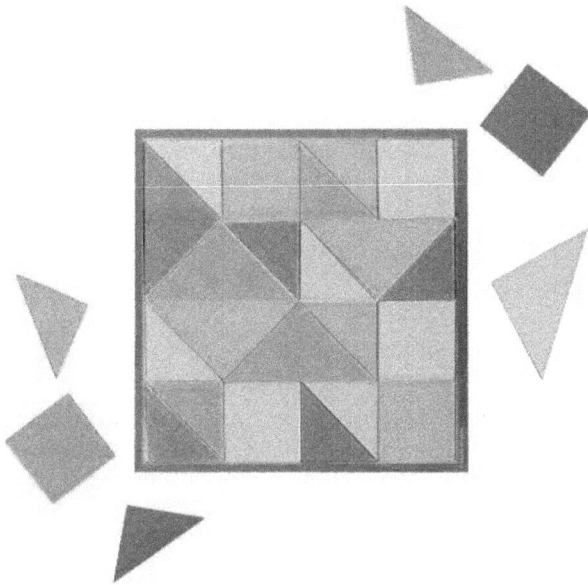

Figure 10.2 Shapes Up Game. *Source*: The Shapes Up game is produced by Educational Insights at https://www.educationalinsights.com/product/shapes+up--174-.do.

I was amazed! We are currently taking our time getting them ready for publication and consulting with college and university mathematicians along the way.

Later, her insight and overall proof form for the classic unsolved problem, the *Collatz Conjecture*, will be presented. Prior to that, however, we will begin to describe some of her exceptional spatial talent and her reflections upon it.

The game *Shapes Up* is a spatial game. As shown in Figure 10.2, you have to fit pieces of different sizes and shapes to complete a large square shape. One constraint: two pieces of the same color cannot touch along a side. They can only touch at a corner.

During the game, as you gather your pieces to complete your square, there comes a time when you may be given an opportunity to quickly rearrange your pieces, by using a timer, so they all fit. It is during this opportunity that Colleen amazed her fellow gamers by speedily rearranging all of her pieces without hesitation and without correction to win the game. This amazing feat was witnessed by four other people—with their jaws dropped.

In contrast to the teens who have been discussed, Colleen was able to articulate several important things about her experience. As she described, "I had to not think." She knew that she could properly arrange all the pieces, but she did not consciously know how to do it. She had to get out of her own way. In other words, her conscious mind needed to be inhibited so that unconscious processes were allowed to take over. Colleen was able to self-inhibit in this way without the help of a stroke, dementia, or mild electrical stimulation on her left frontotemporal area. Thank goodness, Colleen, can do this without disease or brain trauma.

Perhaps, our spatially talented teens do not suffer the temptation to consciously think about the spatial puzzles in front of them. Perhaps, they do not yet need to learn to self-inhibit in this manner. Or maybe, they are not yet able to notice the difference between conscious thinking and unconscious processing. We do not yet know.

EXCEPTIONAL MATH TALENT

Colleen has also an exceptional math talent that she just discovered recently. She says that she has been bored most of her life. By that, she means that despite being exceptionally busy, she was mentally under-stimulated. Then, she found math as an adult and it helped her reveal the full capacity of her amazing gifts. She never liked math in school and attended about one year of college—although she completed several professional certifications, took an occasional college class and professional training class related to her work, as well as adult education classes that interested her. She worked at several investment and financial companies, before working at a major financial institution. Her talent for problem solving was recognized and she moved up to work on some of the company's very difficult problems. She solved them easily and her boredom (or, under-stimulation) continued.

Finally, after an early retirement, a friend one day in 2017 challenged her to focus on an unsolved math problem. "That hasn't been solved?" Colleen exclaimed. "I know how to solve it." She thought the math world, in general, would have been further along than it was. In fact, in school, her teachers never made her aware that there were any unsolved math problems. She began to focus on math while still guiding her younger child into full independence. She conducted her math explorations in her own style and initially did not know much of the math jargon she would find in math books.

Colleen's real challenge was not in actually solving these classic problems. Her struggle was in communicating what she saw in her mind so others could understand her. The answer was before her mind fully formed as a whole. Communicating it required finding an entry point through which to linearly lay it out so others could build it up in their minds piece by piece.

Colleen described her process as a two-stage translation process. First, she has to translate all the relationships that she visualizes into English. Second, she has to translate English into math notation. For Colleen, the translation process is far more laborious than just seeing the solution—which she describes as instantaneous once she fully understands the problem.

She describes the first step of the translation process as constructing a clay-mation movie. Colleen explains it in the following terms. "I have to freeze the image, decide which angle to focus on, which piece of motion and change needs to be captured, write it out, look at the image again to see if I left out anything between the observed change of motion and what I wrote, and do it over then over again. I also have to figure out if I've described enough of the scene for another person to see it. It's hard to see where something which is inherent in what I've written and is obvious to me may not be obvious to anyone else. I regularly have to go back and read through it again in English to see what I may have described in one way in some frames but described in a different way in another set of frames later on."

"After all of that is done, I have to go back and translate it into math linguistics as best I can. This is the most frustrating part because I'm still at such a deficit with the mathematical tools commonly used."

It is like trying to describe a scene that is so vivid and full in your own mind. You have to break it down and construct a pathway using language so that others can build it up part by part and aspect by aspect. But what if there were no pieces and aspects when the answer came to you? You see the elephant in its wholeness and now you have to describe it to a room full of blindfolded people. At these times, language seems so primitive and inadequate for the job.

The task of communicating can be maddening, as can the task of trying to understand the starts and stops of one who is trying to break apart what never really had parts. For Colleen's solution of the *Collatz Conjecture* (described below), I sat with her in face-to-face meetings for about 26 hours over several months and that does not include the 100 plus pages she faxed me to examine.

The process was both exasperating and exhilarating, and it took the experience I had talking with John about metal puzzles to a whole new level. Again, I could understand words, phrases, and some sentences. We humans are so proud of our language—and powerful indeed it is—but there are times when its inadequacy is palpable, even painful. What we are describing has no order of before and after, but the mere act of describing it jams it into a linear order of presenting one thing before another.

I have had several math students who have been accused of cheating by other math teachers. They knew the right answer but could not explain their reasoning. They must have cheated, right? Possibly. But, in my math class, these same students knew the answers to several problems that they performed in front of me with no interaction with anyone near them or any online search (and no answers from the back of the book). I believe there is another explanation. Possibly, they just "saw" the answer and did not have access to the underlying processes that produced it. There were no parts to latch onto to linearize in language. It was all whole and simultaneous for them.

When I work with numbers in my mind, I image them from the perspective of them being outside of myself in a number line or a two-dimensional graph. In other words, I use allocentric coordinates to describe something out there in front of me. Colleen, on the other hand, seems to work in egocentric coordinates. She is in the midst of the numbers and relationships. She says she can turn around in her mind and see the numbers behind her and see how they are related to the numbers in front of her.

While working with Colleen, she would fax me many pages of tables with little to no connecting text to explain how to move through the relationships expressed in the tables. She merely saw all these relationships and knew them to be true. Proving something mathematically was initially foreign to her. A proof must start somewhere and linearly move to a conclusion, but Colleen did not think this way. It was frustrating for her to try to speak in this linear proof language. It was frustrating for me to try to translate these many relationships into a linear story that ultimately constructed the whole that Colleen envisioned.

After I would struggle for days to create a linear math proof from her first fax, Colleen would then fax me a new many-paged fax that presented another set of relationships in another attempt to show what she saw. These relationships were different but related to the first fax. I then had to try again and decide which fax I should give priority to or how the two faxes were related. Colleen has gotten much better at this since I first met her. But I hope learning this ability does not hinder her initial ability to envision all the relationships simultaneously as a whole.

COLLATZ CONJECTURE

No one has proved the *Collatz Conjecture* since it was first proposed some 80 years ago. No one until Colleen, that is. The description of the problem is pretty straightforward but it has stumped some of the most famous mathematicians.

Start with a positive number. If it is odd, then perform 3 times the number and add 1 (3n + 1). If it is even then divide by 2. Keep repeating this. Do all numbers end up in the same place? For example, start with 7, which is odd so it becomes 22. The sequence for 7 by following these two rules is: 22, 11, 34, 17, 52, 26, 13, 40, 20, 10, 5, 16, 8, 4, 2, 1, 4, 2, 1, 4, 2, 1. Once you reach 1, then the sequence enters an infinite loop of 4, 2, 1. So, the important question is: Do all positive numbers no matter where you start always reach 1? The mathematician Collatz conjectured that every number you started with always reached 1. No counterexample has ever been found, but in the 80 years since Collatz proposed this, no one has proved that it has to always work.

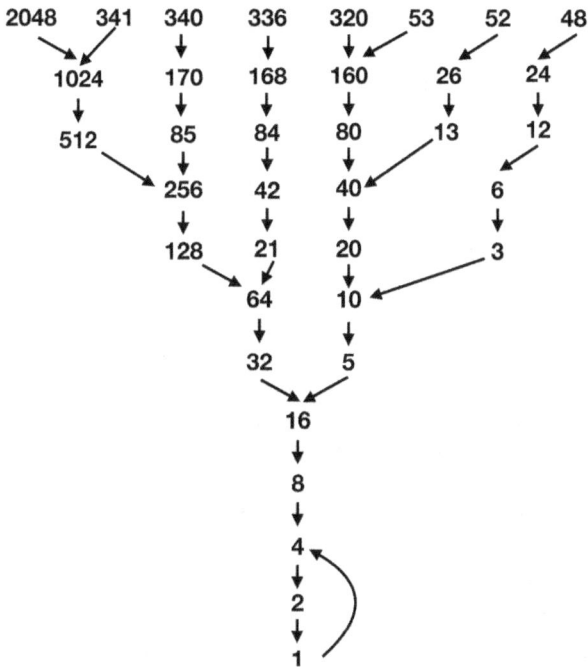

Figure 10.3 Small Sample of the Collatz Tree. *Source*: The author drew this figure and gives permission to Rowman & Littlefield to reprint it.

Figure 10.3 shows a small part of a tree graph that forms from the Collatz rules. Following the arrows, 5 goes to 16 (i.e., 3 × 5 + 1) and 10 goes to 5 (10/2 = 5).

Paul Erdos, the most prolific mathematician of the twentieth century said, "Mathematics may not be ready for such problems" (Lagarias, 2010, p. 4). But Colleen is about to publish a proof on ArXiv.org, a place for electronic pre-prints. We will see if it withstands the scrutiny of the mathematical community.

One aspect of Colleen's spatial abilities is how she can envision numbers. She is not limited to envisioning physical spaces and items within those spaces. Although our visual system has been trained with an incredible amount of visual information about physical space and moving through it, the notion of space is broader than physical space. Our brain can also deal with space more generally. Numbers and how they relate to each other can form a space. The simplest versions may be a number line and a Cartesian coordinate system. Math, however abstract it seems, often resides with the notion of a space: metric space, topological space, Hausdorff space, etc. It seems that the brain can learn to deal spatially with anything that has entities and some relations among those entities. The notion of space seems to flow from this construction and the brain can apply its understanding of space to it.

However, some of us like Colleen can envision numbers quite flexibly in a spatial sense. Others, like me, are quite confined to how numbers are currently spatialized—until Colleen broadens our thinking.

Colleen deals with numbers as though they have two states: as a particle and as a wave. This particle-wave duality is reminiscent of physics, specifically quantum mechanics, in that each particle can also be described as a wave.

For Colleen, when a number acts like a particle, it is static and fixed. The number 7, for example, in its particle form is just a regular 7 that sits on a number line between 6 and 8. The number line spatializes 7 in a familiar way. But from a wave perspective, the number 7 is on the move depending on what came before it and what comes after it. In the *Collatz Conjecture*, 22 comes after 7 and the progression of the wave, as seen above, is 7, 22, 11, 34, 17, 52, 26, 13, 40, 20, 10, 5, 16, 8, 4, 2, 1, 4, 2, 1, 4, 2, 1. In the case of 7, can anything precede it? Yes, 14 can because it is even and dividing by 2 reaches 7. However, no positive number less than 7 can reach 7: 1 goes to 4, 2 goes to 1, 3 goes to 10, 4 goes to 2, 5 goes to 16, 6 goes to 3.

Colleen's intuition about envisioning numbers as waves combined with her spatial ability allowed her to picture the trajectories of the numbers as their waves moved about in the mathematical space determined by the Collatz rules. Whereas some of the top mathematicians only saw disorder, Colleen saw all the waves falling into three distinct categories. Show that each of the three categories of numbers must reach 1 and you have shown that starting with any positive number will reach 1. That is the structure of Colleen's proof.

When Colleen works on a different problem, then the number 7 will be part of a new wave that will depend on what precedes 7 and what follows it. The relations surrounding 7 change, so the wave that 7 is a part of and the space that Colleen envisions changes.

Colleen possessed this deep intuition as a very young girl. When being interviewed for kindergarten, the teacher asked, "How high can you count?" Young Colleen was a bit dumbfounded because she did not know if the teacher wanted her to count by 1's as in 1, 2, 3, 4... Or, by 4's or 7's. She didn't know if the teacher wanted her to count backward from 100 (i.e., count by 1's, 3's, etc.). In that case, should Colleen start at 100 and go backward or should start at 1,000 and go backward? It was not clear to Colleen which way to count. In other words, she did not know which wave to travel on as she moved through the numbers. She did not rigidly assume counting only meant starting at 1 and going up by one each time. After some awkwardness and questions by Colleen, the teacher realized that Colleen was very skilled and could count in any way that the teacher desired.

Mathematics is now ready for such problems as the *Collatz Conjecture* and Colleen's methods will help us understand more of the mathematical world. She has proofs to other famous unsolved problems that soon will be available for the mathematical community to scrutinize and enjoy.

SUMMARY

Lisa, a teen, has extraordinary spatial skills and like other talented teens I have encountered (e.g., Steven) struggles to articulate anything about what occurs when she uses her gift. Colleen, an adult, has had more experience living with her gift and is able to share some insightful comments about how she relates to it. The trick might be to get a talented youth to relate to their gift more consciously without damaging or stifling the gift.

The experience of Colleen in school suggests that there are probably other children who have a different relationship with numbers, but schooling forces upon children a rigid way of conceiving of and spatializing them. Colleen's current and imminent contributions to mathematics, by solving multiple classic unsolved problems, suggest that there are other promising ways to relate to and spatialize numbers. She lives within them, so to speak, and watches how they move around in waves. And the waves change as the problem changes. Hopefully, Colleen's influence will help us discover youth who relate to numbers differently before they are forced to view them in particular rigid manner.

REFERENCES

Lagarias, J. C. (2010). *The ultimate challenge: The 3x + 1 problem.* American Mathematical Society.

Chapter 11

Linguistic Math Puzzles

INTRODUCTION

In this chapter, we focus on math puzzles that have a spatial aspect but also require a fair amount of language to understand them. There are students, Dennis and Connor (both pseudonyms), who are attracted to puzzles that require language to name the relevant constraints.

As we conclude by showcasing the exceptional abilities of these two students, it is interesting to observe what types of puzzles each student is drawn to work on. Some students wanted purely physical puzzles (e.g., entangled metal puzzles). Other students of mine seemed drawn to spatial puzzles on paper, in which they had to do the manipulations in their minds. Some wanted puzzles in which the stated goal was the only language needed. Others were content with linguistically taking in the constraints (e.g., "You cannot do this move" and "You can only do this type of move"). Future research needs to pay careful attention to these differences as we continue to dissect and articulate the diversity of stellar gifts in our youth.

In the next section, we will also begin to analyze what makes a particular math puzzle difficult and tricky. Solving a math puzzle often requires going against certain ways that humans tend to group things together, as articulated by Gestalt psychologists. Of course, there are probably youth who do not group things together in the ways described by Gestalt psychologists. In fact, Dennis, the youth featured in the next section, may be one of those people. However, further investigation is needed to confirm or disconfirm this possibility.

GAUSS AND DENNIS

Carl Friedrich Gauss (1777–1855) was one of the most famous mathematicians of all time and has many mathematical things named after him. The story goes that when Gauss was ten years old, his teacher wanted to punish the class so he had them add up all the numbers between 1 and 100. $1 + 2 + 3 + 4 + 5 + 6$ and on and on. This task should have taken a long time, perhaps hours. After a few minutes, however, young Gauss put down his writing instrument and the teacher went over to check on him. Gauss had found a pattern and had written down the correct answer!

I gave my first-year high school students (14 years olds) this same problem, including Dennis (a pseudonym). Along with the way the problem is described above, I also gave my students a visual form of the problem (Figure 11.1). A three-row triangle of coins has six total coins and is like adding together $1 + 2 + 3 = 6$. Similarly, a four-row triangle of coins has ten coins and is like adding together $1 + 2 + 3 + 4 = 10$. Without building a coin triangle with 100 rows, determine how many coins would be in a 100-row triangle. What is the pattern as to how the number of coins grows as the triangle gets more rows of coins? Can this pattern be expressed in a way that will work for any number of rows?

Dennis returned the next morning saying that he noticed a pattern and that on his long bus ride the previous night he did many calculations in his head to check if his pattern worked. It always did! So, Dennis excitedly wrote a little formula on the board and my jaw dropped open. The young man standing in front of me had written down the same formula that the prodigy, genius Gauss had found when he was ten years old.

None of the other students got very close to finding the pattern. They tried triangles with many different number of rows but came up with no formula that could calculate the number of coins for any size triangle.

Dennis had made the same leap that Carl Gauss had made. If you cannot find a pattern with the numbers you are adding together; then, counterintuitively, add up even more of them! It seems strange to do more work by

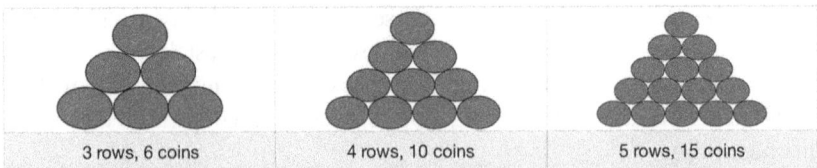

| 3 rows, 6 coins | 4 rows, 10 coins | 5 rows, 15 coins |

Figure 11.1 Visually Counting an Increasing Sequence of Numbers. *Source:* The author drew this figure and gives permission to Rowman & Littlefield to reprint it.

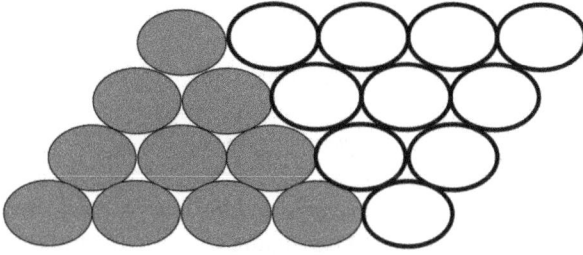

Figure 11.2 Counting Up Twice as Many Coins. *Source*: The author drew this figure and gives permission to Rowman & Littlefield to reprint it.

1	2	3	4	5	6	7	8	9 ... 100
100	**99**	**98**	**97**	**96**	**95**	**94**	**93**	**92** ... **1**
101	101	101	101	101	101	101	101	101 101

Figure 11.3 Gauss's Original Way of Solving the Problem. *Source*: The author drew this figure and gives permission to Rowman & Littlefield to reprint it.

adding together more numbers; but, really, you end up doing far less work. For example, as in Figure 11.2, the dark triangle on the left has four rows and a total of 10 coins. If we place an identical triangle next to the original one and flip it, then we have 20 total coins, which is twice the number we want. But look at the pattern that forms! Combining the two triangles forms a shape that has four rows and each row now has the same number of coins: five. So, 4 times 5 is 20, which is twice the number of the original triangle, so just divide by two to get the correct answer of ten!

You can easily convince yourself that setting two identical triangles of coins next to each other in this flipped way always produces a pattern that has the same number of coins in each row. In the case of 100 rows, there are 101 coins in each row. Multiply 100 by 101 and divide by 2 to get 5,050.

The evidence is that young Gauss solved this problem in a non-visual manner. As in Figure 11.3, write the numbers from left to right on one line starting from 1 and moving toward 100. Then, reverse the order of the next line starting from 100 on the left and moving to the right toward 1.

We wanted 1 to 100. Figure 11.3 shows we have 1 to 100 twice. If we add together the two numbers that are on top of each, then each pair of numbers, each column, adds up to 101. How many 101's do we have? 100 of them. So, 101 times 100 gives you twice as much as you need. Divide by 2 to get the final answer of 5,050.

COUNTERINTUITIVE MENTAL MANEUVERS

Solving this problem, like Gauss and Dennis did, requires several unnatural or counterintuitive moves to frame the problem properly. First, adding together more numbers than are initially given to you (e.g., 1 to 100) goes against the sense of efficiency, which might be expressed as "Don't do more work than you need to." Also, against a sense of simplicity, as in "Don't make the work more complex than necessary." Also, against a sense of straightforwardness, as in "Don't be circuitous, but solve the problem directly."

To see more coins than the original triangle, you need to zoom out to expose more of the open space around the triangle of coins. Figure 11.4a shows the original triangle with a box closely around it to show that we are zoomed in to focus on the coins of the triangle. Notice that the triangle is centered within the surrounding box (i.e., area of attention and focus). This indicates that when we focus on something it is usually in the center of our field of vision. If we zoom out to show more of the surrounding space, as in Figure 11.4b, notice that we have backed up in a straight manner so that the triangle is still centered. This way of zooming out is very natural for us because it keeps the triangle in the center of our field of vision and thus, our attention. However, we need to zoom out as in Figure 11.4c, which opens up more space to one side of the triangle leaving the triangle uncentered. After this sequence of unusual moves, Figure 11.4d shows the result of these moves: zoom-out, left-shift, double, flip, and juxtapose.

Of course, the mental operations may not happen in this manner. An individual may just experience starting with Figure 11.4a and moving directly to Figure 11.4d, without being aware of any intermediate steps. Figure 11.4 merely indicates a possible sequence for simulating how Figure 11.4d might be reached from Figure 11.4a. Each of the proposed maneuvers—zooming out, zooming out uncentered, adding a second figure that is flipped—is counterintuitive to undertake. Left to our own devices, we would usually remain at Figure 11.4a and just focus and think about those coins.

Further, humans have a preference for symmetry (Rock, 1985) and examining the initial triangle of coins yields a simple symmetry on each side of

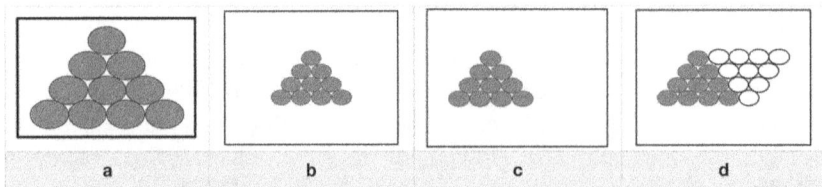

Figure 11.4   Zooming Out in an Unusual Way. *Source:* The author drew this figure and gives permission to Rowman & Littlefield to reprint it.

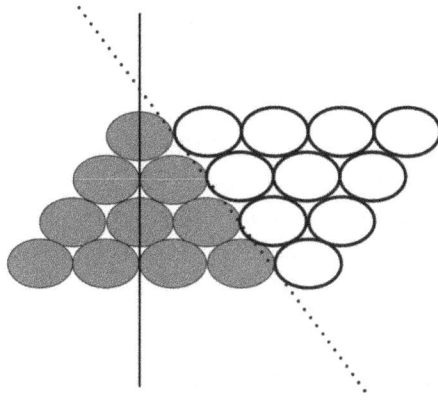

Figure 11.5 Symmetries in the Visual Form of the Coins. *Source*: The author drew this figure and gives permission to Rowman & Littlefield to reprint it.

the vertical line in Figure 11.5. The presence of this symmetry can lull us into complacency and stop us from searching for a more unusual symmetry that is needed to solve the problem. In this case, the relevant symmetry comes from the angled dotted line between the original upright triangle and the flipped triangle.

CONCLUSIONS ABOUT DENNIS

The Gestalt principles (e.g., symmetry and simplicity) give us clues as to how most people prefer to group things together and proceed when problem-solving. This list of principles gives us a good list to actively counteract when we are solving problems. Quite possibly, something is a problem because our inclination for simplicity implicitly hinders us from adding together more numbers than we were initially given. Or, our preference for certain types of symmetry inhibit us from seeing other kinds of symmetry—or perhaps, settling for asymmetry.

Further, perhaps some youth are not bound by these Gestalt principles and they move against them effortlessly because, for them, they are not there.

In any case, future research and observation will engage in two tasks. First, when analyzing a puzzle, does seeing the solution require going against one of the Gestalt principles? Second, are there students who are not inhibited by one or more of the Gestalt principles and, thus, is their thinking more flexible and free?

In the next section, we consider Connor, who solved a classically difficult math puzzle in just five minutes.

EULER AND CONNOR

Leonhard Euler (1707–1783) was the most prolific mathematician of all time. The story goes that the folks in the Prussian city of Konigsberg would take their walks across the series of bridges in Figure 11.6 over a particular section of the Pregel River. The question arose as to whether a citizen could take a walk that would cross each of the bridges exactly once. You can start anywhere you want and end anywhere. You just have to cross each of the bridges just once. No one had found such a path but that does not mean that one does not exist.

If you do not like thinking about bridges, Figure 11.7 has the same problem; only using hallways instead of river banks, rooms instead of islands, and doorways instead of bridges. Other than that, it is structurally the same problem. Can a student take a walk that goes through each of the doorways exactly once? Again, the student can start anywhere and end anywhere.

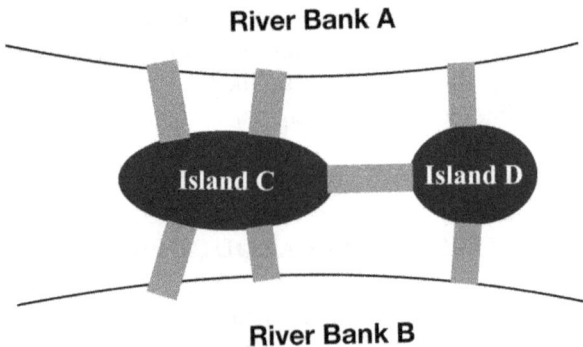

Figure 11.6   Konigsberg Bridge Problem. *Source*: The author drew this figure and gives permission to Rowman & Littlefield to reprint it.

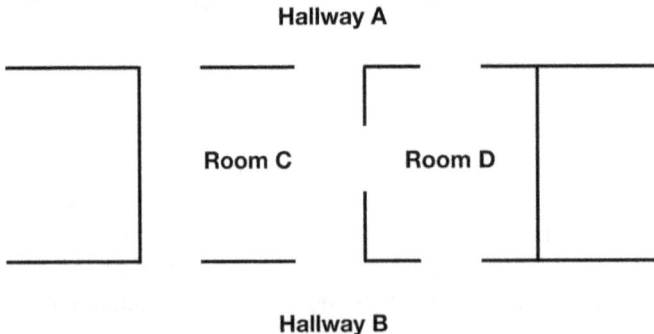

Figure 11.7   Konigsberg Building Problem. *Source*: The author drew this figure and gives permission to Rowman & Littlefield to reprint it.

I have given this problem to many classes of students over the years. Students work on it diligently trying pathway after pathway. After much effort, many of them sense that it is not possible to find such a pathway. One student came to the conclusion that it was impossible but kept trying because he mistakenly believed that a teacher would never give students a problem that did not have a solution. Wrong! The interesting thing about this problem is why it is impossible.

Then, in 2017, I gave it to Connor's (a pseudonym) class and Connor determined that it was impossible within about five minutes. More than that, Connor named the precise reason it was impossible—the same reason that Euler articulated and proved back in 1735.

Like other students, Connor first examined several possible pathways, but then became suspicious and switched gears. Connor counted the number of bridges from each land mass—as in the Figure 11.8.

Noticing that the number of bridges coming from each land mass was odd, Connor quickly wondered how many odd numbers would cause a problem.

He removed a bridge/doorway between Land/Room C and Land/Room D and recalculated the number of bridges/doorways, as in Figure 11.9. With this removal, we are now down to just two odd numbers of bridges/doorways. It is fairly easy to see that you can now make a journey that will use each bridge/door. Here is just one of the possible journeys: A to C to B to C to A to D to B.

Since the bridge problem and the doorway problem are really the same problem, we are essentially focusing on the connectivity. Euler found a way to visualize the connectivity and get rid of the irrelevant details about land, bridges, room, doors, etc. The left panel of Figure 11.10 shows the original *Konigsberg Bridge Problem* as a bare graph of connections without any particular details. Instead of land masses, we now have what are called *nodes*. Instead of bridges, we now have *links*.

The right panel of Figure 11.10 shows the graph when we removed one of the bridges/doorways as in Figure 11.9.

Connor was able to come to the conclusion within five minutes that it was impossible to make such a journey for any graph that had more than two nodes with an odd number of links. Some other students had a hunch that it

Land Masses	Bridges
A	3, odd
B	3, odd
C	5, odd
D	3, odd

Figure 11.8 Number of Bridges from Each Land Mass.

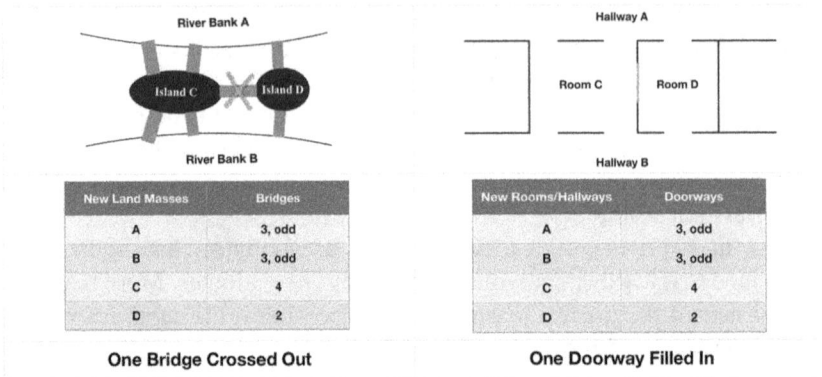

Figure 11.9 New Maps and Tables with Corresponding Bridge/Doorway Removed. *Source*: The author drew this figure and gives permission to Rowman & Littlefield to reprint it.

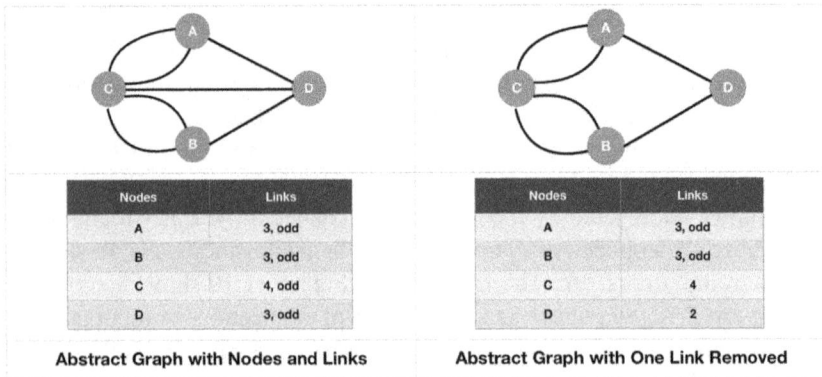

Figure 11.10 Abstracting the Connectivity to Form a General Graph. *Source*: The author drew this figure and gives permission to Rowman & Littlefield to reprint it.

was impossible and their reason had something to do with the odd number of links. Only Connor, however, came to a certain conclusion and had named the precise reason. Of course, Euler also mathematically proved that this journey was impossible for graphs with more than two odd numbers. Still, Connor's insight and reasoning were quite impressive!

CONCLUSIONS ABOUT CONNOR

The amazing thing is that Connor solved this classic problem and he has been diagnosed with a learning disability in math and ADHD. Further, Connor's math grades over the years were mostly C's and D's, with just one A and two B's in the last few years of school.

One thing that is impressive is Connor's executive functioning. Quickly, he switched approaches from looking for a solution to searching for why it might be impossible. Second, Connor used effective analysis to move from a suspicion that it might have to do with odd numbers of bridges to devising a way to check out his hunch. He flexibly played with the bridge diagram and removed a bridge so that now there were only two odd numbers.

Third, he was able to generalize quickly that the problem was having more than two landmasses with an odd number of bridges. Although Connor did not rigorously prove it, as Euler did, he reasoned well and convinced himself that it had to be the case. Finally, Connor generalized quickly from working on the bridge diagram to working on any structure that had the same connectivity. When given the problem with rooms and hallways, he immediately said that this was the same as the bridge problem.

If Connor had lived in the 1700s, he may have beaten Euler to solving the bridge problem and creating a whole new branch of mathematics called *Graph Theory*.

REFERENCE

Rock, I. (1985). *The logic of perception.* Cambridge, MA: MIT Press.

Chapter 12

Conclusions and Next Steps

Many exceptional abilities in humans are escaping detection. Further, many learning and comprehension issues have not been understood precisely enough to craft successful counter-techniques. One reason is that current cognitive theories have an insufficient number of categories to describe the true diversity of human cognition. Second, current theories are not grounded and integrated well enough with the latest neuroscience findings.

Infinite Learning Diversity has an astronomical number of possible categories by combining the unlimited number of features that humans can detect, the many ways we can group them, the many ways to blend/unify them, and several ways to attend to them. Each human can exhibit a unique combination of strengths and weaknesses within this fine-grained system.

One avenue that we explored was to test these many possible abilities using as little language as possible so as to try to get beneath, as much as possible, the veneer of language to reach our underlying non-linguistic abilities. This book articulated the beginning of a progression of puzzles that started with purely non-linguistic ones and then slowly moved to ones that required more and more language to explain their goal and constraints.

More research is necessary to complete this progression from puzzles that animals can solve to ones that only language-wielding humans (or linguistically trained animals such as Koko the gorilla) can solve. Pinpointing the moment in the puzzle progression where language becomes absolutely necessary will help us understand the minimal task that a linguistic human can solve but a non-linguistic animal cannot: the simplest cognitive task for which language becomes absolutely necessary.

Another avenue we explored was to conceive of the task of understanding language as a transformation from language to a mental simulation. A mental simulation re-uses many of the same brain areas that are used if the person was actually experiencing what the language described.

Words and grammatical constructs are viewed as a loose set of instructions for constructing an appropriate mental simulation. Understanding text means that a person can construct an appropriate mental simulation that allows them to answer questions and infer implications. The meaning of the text can be construed as the mental simulation as it is experienced by a human.

When a person names features and associations of words and descriptions, this can help researchers understand that person's profile of what senses and features they strongly prefer. Redescribing a scene using a film director's language can also reveal much about the strengths, weaknesses, and preferences involved in constructing mental simulations. Trying to match grammatical constructs with their corresponding film director's terms (e.g., pan, zoom, and cut) can shed much insight into various comprehension issues that a person might have.

NEXT STEPS: LET'S GET STARTED!

The *Infinite Learning Diversity* Diversity approach holds a great deal of promise but needs much testing and refinement. It has already helped me uncover some hidden abilities in my students, even before the framework was fully articulated. When it becomes more systematically applied, I am hopeful that many exceptional abilities will be discovered in our youth. I am also highly optimistic that its application will help pinpoint some currently mysterious learning and language comprehension issues and then help devise how to deal with them effectively.

Again, I invite any interested teacher, administrator, parent, student advocate, student, or researcher to become part of this journey of discovery into the hidden abilities of our youth. Please contact me if you would like to be part of this exciting endeavor that stems from the *Infinite Learning Diversity* approach. Or, contact me if you would like me to be a part of your work to discover, develop, and advocate for the amazing cognitive diversity of our youth.

Email: tmccaffrey@eaglehill.school

Index

allocentric and egocentric coordinates, 91, 100

animal cognition: "Beak and Brain" documentary about, 84; diverse species puzzles in, ix; Grandin problem-solving speculation in, 19; non-immediate future planning in, 23–24; non-verbal puzzles use in, 83; puzzle physical cause-effect structure in, 83–84; rewards for, 84; study of, ix

Are We Smart Enough to Know How Smart Animals Are? (de Waal), ix

Armstrong, T., 1–3

Bar, Moshe, 24

"Beak and Brain" documentary, 84

Beeman, Mark, 49, 56

blending: chimp and peanut exercise in, 15; as cognitive science central tenet, 7, 30; default-mode network in, 29; eyelets in high-top basketball shoe in, 9; feedback and feedforward connections in, 28; Grandin on, 17–18; hippocampal-cortical system in, 28; image awareness in, 18; individual differences in, 18; inner world of images in, 16; language domination in, 18; language-suppression technique for, 16–17; mammal in, 7, 30; neural activity operations in, 55–56, 57; nocturnal replay in, 29; past and present trap in, 18; perception and memory ability in, 7–8; rat maze learning in, 29; reverse triangle problem in, 27, 27–28; sense and nonsense in, 41; sensorimotor system in, 29; two images in, 27; visual perception and visual imagery in, 28. *See also* Conceptual Blending theory

brain, human, 59; anticipatory neural activity in, 24; Broca's and Wernicke's areas in, 35, 48; confirmed predictions in, 24; cortex language comprehension involvement in, 48; language processing in, 34; memory as reconstructive process in, 25; neural activities and linear expression in, 40–41; prediction and memory and attention focus in, 24; remembering and imagining in, 25; space notion of, 101–2; trauma in, 35, 43; visual and motor system coordination in, 36. *See also* neural activity

About the Author

Tony McCaffrey holds a doctorate in cognitive psychology and teaches at Eagle Hill School in Hardwick, Massachusetts—a school for teens with learning differences. He has noticed some exceptional abilities in his students that had been overlooked in their academic and neuropsychological files. So, Tony began to develop a new framework, *Infinite Learning Diversity*, which is a wider net for better detecting these amazing abilities. He hopes his work can help all students come to know their true potential by uncovering their skills that often go unnoticed. Tony and his wife Stephanie live in the beautiful New England town of West Brookfield, Massachusetts.

www.ingramcontent.com/pod-product-compliance
Lightning Source LLC
Chambersburg PA
CBHW030654270326
41929CB00007B/358